W9-BUK-150

"Completing twelve Ironman races around the world, including five Hawaii Ironman World Championships, takes guts, discipline, drive, and passion. *Make Big Happen!* is a powerful read with valuable lessons that will allow you to *make BIG happen* in your life."

—**Heather Fuhr,** Ironman World Champion, fifteen-time Ironman champion, Ironman Hall of Fame inductee, and Triathlon Canada Hall of Fame inductee

"If you are tired of sitting on the sidelines and want to become the best, you need to have passion, courage, and commitment to train and be coached by the best. Mark Moses has made it happen in business, sport, and life. If you are committed to making big happen in your life, this book is for you."

—**Anthony Davis,** ex-NFL player, College All-American, and five-time national champion in football and baseball at University of Southern California, Los Angeles, California

"Mark Moses is one of the hardest working guys I know, and, unlike many entrepreneurs, he spends time in the trenches, puts his nose to the grindstone, and combines seriously impressive business achievements with huge personal feats that include twelve Ironman triathlons. There's no fluff, only practical tips that Mark has proven to work."

—**Ben Greenfield,** *New York Times* bestselling author

"As a friend, I've watched Mark Moses live out everything he reveals to you in *Make Big Happen!* It focuses on a very few simple concepts and real-life stories of success that you can relate to. This book will be transformational. Get ready to make BIG happen in your own life!"

—**Henry McGovern,** CEO, AmRest (Pizza Hut, KFC, Burger King, Starbucks, Blue Frog, La Tagliatella)

"Mark Moses is an energetic entrepreneur from a small town in Canada who made it big—and shares with you how you can do the same—while giving much back in the process. Mark is a great 'student' of business with a passion for helping his fellow entrepreneurs. His practical approaches and questions are golden."

—**Verne Harnish,** founder, Entrepreneurs' Organization,
author of *Scaling Up (Rockefeller Habits 2.0)*

"When I first met Mark Moses, my company was on the verge of bankruptcy, and I had to convince him to take me on as a client. In a few short years my company's profits and sales had grown exponentially while my quality of life improved and stress decreased. Mark is an outstanding coach who helped me grow my company from a hundred million to over a *billion* dollars in sales. He definitely knows how to *Make Big Happen!*"

—**Rich Balot,** founder and executive chairman,
A Wireless—Verizon Wireless Premium Retailer

"Unlike so many books based on complex concepts, my friend Mark Moses has lived out the four simple Make Big Happen Questions™ he will share with you in this book. *Make Big Happen!* is short on theory and long on real-world success stories from Mark's own life and from the lives of many CEOs who have built amazing businesses because of his guidance. Read Mark's book and prepare to *make BIG happen* in your own life."

—**Chuck Blakeman,** author of #1 Business Book
of the Year; speaker and founder, Crankset Group

"Inspiring. Funny. Touching. Mark Moses delivers an important and invaluable "how-to manual" on using your head and your heart to succeed in business and in life. *Make Big Happen!* is an entertaining read whose insights and teachings are simple to understand and implement, powerful in their results, and proven through real-world experience. Mark has created a must-read for any business leader who wants to be better, do better, and live better!"

—Michael Maas, CEO, Solutions 2 Go

"Self-help books are a dime a dozen, but good ones are rare. *Make Big Happen!* is based on real-life stories that you can apply instantly. Get ready to *make BIG happen* in your own life!"

—Steve Acorn, president, Student Painters

"Mark Moses is an incredibly successful and influential entrepreneur and CEO coach. His formula for success is both rare and highly valuable for any entrepreneur who wants to think big, act big, and achieve beyond their own expectations. He simplifies issues that others see as complex and focuses your thinking to act on the most important levers that really make all the difference. Mark has been a powerful influence on taking my own entrepreneurial career to a whole new level of performance."

—Anthony Venus, CEO and cofounder, YayPay

"*Make Big Happen!* is a generous gift to entrepreneurs and CEOs. Mark Moses has distilled his decades of business success into a practical and actionable book that is filled with real stories of how to *make BIG happen*. At times quite touching, Mark doesn't hold back on the challenges along the entrepreneurial journey, and he always offers an inspiring way to overcome them."

—Steve Sanduski, CFP®, president, Belay Advisor, and *New York Times* bestselling author

"When I met Mark Moses, my business had opportunities, but I didn't know how to execute. His insight and coaching opened my eyes to strategies to grow my business in ways I never thought possible. If you're serious about scaling your business while living life to the fullest, *Make Big Happen!* is for you. Don't just read it, live it."

—Nathan Mersereau, CFP®,
president, Planning Alternatives

"You don't need to reinvent the wheel. You don't need to figure it out all by yourself. If you really want to build your business and *make BIG happen*, then read this book and learn from Mark Moses, the guy who really knows how to *make BIG happen!*"

—Jason Reid, CEO, National Services Group

"I've worked with Mark Moses for years, and I can confidently say that making big happen is what Mark is all about. With Mark as my CEO coach, we've more than doubled the size of our company, and with our recent closing of a large round of institutional capital, we're just getting started. Mark preaches exactly what he has successfully practiced: religiously consistent application of the fundamentals—clear goals, planning, execution, measurement, adjustment, etc. His remarkable career as an entrepreneur, with epic highs and some crushing lows, gives him a perspective that's both practical and inspirational. He will definitely challenge you to *make BIG happen!*"

—Craig Coleman, CEO, ForwardLine

"Mark Moses shares his concise and actionable ideas to help readers zoom in and take action. This book will save you thousands of dollars in consulting fees. Read it and then do what Mark says. You will definitely see your life begin to shift."

—Mimi Doe, CEO, Top Tier Admissions

"Choosing to work with Mark Moses as my coach was one of the single best decisions I have made in my career. Mark has been instrumental in helping me navigate big structural issues in our business in a thoughtful, deliberate, methodical way. In *Make Big Happen!*, Mark has laid out the principles and strategies he coached me on, and now they're available to all entrepreneurs and CEOs around the world. Don't miss this opportunity."

—Cyrus Sigari, CEO, jetAVIVA

"As the COO of an entrepreneurial business that went from losing money to being sold to an international tech giant, I experienced first-hand Mark's framework of *Make Big Happen!* In the five years Mark worked with our management team, he helped transform the business from a lifestyle business into a recognized market leader with double-digit annual growth. Looking back, it was the relentless execution of The Make Big Happen Questions quarter after quarter that drove our extraordinary results."

—Don Schiavone, COO, Grasshopper

"Mark Moses is a man on a mission and knows how to *make BIG happen!* Learn how to ask the right questions, overcome obstacles, and create the system it will take to finish on top in business and in life. Mark is not only a great athlete, but he has also defied the odds in business multiple times. You will get more and be able to do more as a result of reading this book."

—Wil Smith, CEO, Greenlaw Partners

"Mark Moses does everything *big*, including the impact he makes on others. I've experienced this firsthand—as a client, as a business partner, and as a friend—and if you will follow the guidance offered in *Make Big Happen!*, you will experience it too."

—Sheldon Harris, former president, Cold Stone Creamery

"I have been working with Mark as my business coach for several years and have learned the invaluable lesson that 'things that get measured get done.' Mark has helped my company with his systematic approach of focusing on the specific key activities that will drive results and has helped me and my team *make BIG happen!* This book will help you do the same."

—Kathy Colace, CEO, JBN & Associates

"The first conversation I had with Mark Moses about *Make Big Happen!* was a game changer in my life. I hired Mark, and he taught me the *Make Big Happen!* system and process. Using Mark's system and process, we grew my company dramatically during the worst recession in history, sold the business for a huge multiple, and now I am fortunate to call Mark a great friend, coach, and partner at CEO Coaching International. If you are an entrepreneur and have a burning desire to reach your full potential, then read this book, implement the ideas, and your life will change—for the better."

—David Sobel, principal partner, Home Warranty of America; partner, CEO Coaching International

"As an entrepreneur, thinking big is not a problem, but not stuffing it up is. There are lots of moving parts in any business. Mark's book, *Make Big Happen!*, is a roadmap we have followed over the last fifteen months Mark has coached me. This year we are listed on the BRW Fast 100. Mark has transferred his personal experiences and knowledge into a proven formula to help other entrepreneurs grow to reach their potential.

—Ben Hargraves, managing director, Hargraves Urban

"To know Mark Moses is to know a 'winner.' I have known Mark for over thirty years, and even back in the early days, I knew that he was driven, focused, and would challenge those around him to be better. He has solid business values as well as admirable family values. When you learn how to *make BIG happen*, you will get up to 'Mark' speed or get out of the way."

—**Neil Bradley,** head coach and owner of
Carriers Direct, Inc. and Bradley Transport, Inc.

"Every once in a while someone enters into your life or you read a book that provides you with lessons that can be transformational in the way you look at your business. It's rarer when you can apply those lessons to your life as well. *Make Big Happen!* is one of those books, and Mark Moses is one of those guys. *Make Big Happen!* is a great read with four basic principles of Vision, Action, Anticipation, and Measurement that will set you on the path to accountability and to achieving your goals."

—**Rajeev Kapur,** president and CEO, 1105 Media

"Mark Moses' book, *Make Big Happen!* isn't just educational, it's transformational. Thinking big is not easy, and trying to make big things happen is even more difficult. What Mark has accomplished in his life is remarkable. The stories he shares in the book will help you live a big life."

—**Wei Chen,** first Chinese citizen to fly a
single-engine airplane around the world,
chairman and CEO, Sun Pacific Bank

"Mark Moses is an extraordinary guy and an inspiration to anyone that meets him. He's determined, focused, passionate about helping others, and he's highly respected. In line with the title of his book *Make Big Happen!*, if you are lucky enough to meet Mark in person, you will find him to be bigger than life because of his endless energy and a true commitment to make a difference by making things happen. Mark is a very effective and sincere coach, and I think he is making a great contribution here in sharing his thinking, his process, and his personal experiences with the world."

—**Rob Follows,** founding chairman, Altruvest Charitable Services (BoardMatch®, matching and training talented professionals to serve on charitable boards), founding chairman and CEO, STS Capital Partners, and 7 Summiter (incl. Mt. Everest in 2006)

"Mark Moses' guidance changes lives. Yes, it helps supercharge business results too. What's unique is that it comes from his life and from his family's lives ... from his real world experiences in addition to much research. Great coaches are outstanding learners too. Just like Mark, I hope you invest some of your time in *Make Big Happen!* You and those you influence will be better because you did."

—**Vance Caesar,** PhD, author, *The High Achiever's Guide to Happiness*

"I've known Mark Moses for over fifteen years, and he has shown over and over that he knows how to *make BIG happen*—not only for himself but for those around him. Mark has provided extremely helpful input as I've raised $80M for my current venture and continue to achieve outsized results. Much of what he has said to me personally over the years is now repeated in this book for everyone to benefit from."

—**Josh McCarter,** CEO, Booker.com

"Don't read this book if you are satisfied with mediocrity. But if you are looking to zero in on how to achieve what you truly want in life and business, then reading *Make Big Happen!* is a must. Mark's own experience is enough content for a compelling manuscript. But the real world examples he blends in from clients who have applied The Make Big Happen Questions across industry sectors and businesses drives home that his approach is the roadmap to success you've been searching for."

—Dan Berkon, CEO, Culmen International

"Mark Moses has always dreamed, executed, and created BIG results! Now, he shares his formula with you!"

—Scott Duffy, bestselling author, *Launch*

"It's as if Mark Moses has taken a thousand books on business and distilled them down to the easiest, most succinct points possible. He 'sees' success in its most simple state and makes it a real pleasure to understand. Any businessperson will benefit reading Mark's book!"

—Christopher Coutinho, CEO, Paystar Logistics, Inc.

"Most of the success my company has experienced over the past several years has been attributed to the teachings found in this book and ultimately from Mark Moses holding me accountable. I have grown into a much better leader for my company thanks to Mark and his valuable, no-nonsense strategies. I recommend reading this book for anyone wanting to grow their business and become a better leader."

—Norm Curtis, president and CEO, Keystone Western

"Mark's insight in *Make Big Happen!* is not only profound but real. He did it. Experience trumps theory any day as an entrepreneur."

—**Jo Burston,** founder and CEO, Job Capital
and Inspiring Rare Birds, Sydney, Australia

"It is fun for me to now see that The Make Big Happen Questions from Mark Moses are incorporated in a book for all entrepreneurs and CEOs to benefit from. From my first coaching session with Mark, I have always referred to these as my 'must haves.' Mark, his four questions, and the many hours of his coaching have led me to achieve so many of my personal and professional goals."

—**Sharon Blank,** CEO, Language Scientific

"I am in my fifth year as a coaching client of Mark Moses. We now implement The Make Big Happen Questions on a daily basis and have accomplished things in the past five years that could easily have taken multiple decades to accomplish. *Make Big Happen!* is a wonderful compilation of Mark's experience and process, and I highly recommend this book to anyone who wants to challenge themselves to give, live, and work to their potential."

—**Bill Keen,** founder and CEO, Keen Wealth Advisors

"I am very glad that finally all of Mark's performance and business wisdom is available in a book. I know personally the meaningful impact it had on me. It's a book I'll be sharing often."

—**Andres Jaramillo,** CEO, Don Pedro's
Meat and Tepache Beverages

"There is no such thing as a stupid question. If you don't know the answer, the question is valid. Mark Moses' book perfectly captures that sentiment, and it is something I try and apply at the winery all the time."

—David R. Duncan, president and CEO,
Silver Oak and Twomey Cellars

"I've had the privilege of having Mark Moses as my executive coach. Mark is the world's best executive coach. He's had a big impact on my business and my life. The principles contained in *Make Big Happen!* have helped me grow my business from my parent's spare bedroom to over five thousand global employees."

—Bryce Maddock, CEO, TaskUs

"Mark has taken what he learned from hard lessons and from mentors/partners/peers/fellow entrepreneurs and written a wonderful book that can serve as a success guide for committed entrepreneurs and those who aspire to entrepreneurship. Read it and make notes in the margins. It is a foundational piece that can serve as a roadmap."

—Richard Carr, former CEO, Vistage International

"I've had the pleasure of working with Mark Moses as my executive coach, and I can say without hesitation that he has completely changed my life. Mark has helped me grow my business from $18M to over $100M in revenue in less than five years. In *Make Big Happen!*, Mark combines everything he has learned into a simple and actionable book on business and life success."

—Sheldon Wolitski, CEO and founder, The Select Group

"*Make Big Happen!* is straightforward and hard hitting for the all-go leader. Mark will help you see through the forest and focus on what it takes to succeed at whatever your goals are. He is an expert at creating simple and highly effective strategies to get where you want to go; no shortcuts, just straight to the goal line."

—Rick Stern, CEO, Nitel, Chicago, Illinois

"Mark boils the necessary steps down to their most basic form, making the complex simple. That gift alone is worth the cost of entry. But it doesn't stop there. Through insights and honest dialogue, Moses helps anyone who wants to grow their business define and execute their process."

—Steve Lockshin, Barron's top independent advisor, 2011, 2012, 2013; founder, Advice Period & Partner Betterment Institutional

"Mark has put together an outstanding guide for managing yourself and your company. He's pulled from his considerable experience and has shared insights gleaned from years of highs and lows. This is a must-have book on every CEO's desk."

—Salim Ismail, global ambassador and founding director, Singularity University, Author Exponential Organizations

"Mark Moses is rare in the world of CEO coaching because he actually holds CEOs' feet to the fire more than anyone I know. Holding people accountable for achieving objectives is a rare skill, and Mark has it in spades. Mark's ability to rapidly cut to the heart of virtually any matter gives me chills, since often I don't want to tell him what is really going on. I highly recommend *Make Big Happen!* because it will force you to take the medicine of accountability and execution."

—Rick Sapio, CEO, Mutual Capital Alliance, Inc.

MAKE
BIG
HAPPEN

HOW TO LIVE, WORK, AND GIVE **BIG**

For CEOs, Entrepreneurs, and Leaders

MARK MOSES

ForbesBooks

Published by ForbesBooks, Charleston, South Carolina. Member of Advantage Media Group.

ForbesBooks is a registered trademark, and the ForbesBooks colophon is a trademark of Forbes Media, LLC.

Printed in the United States of America.

ISBN: 978-1-59932-611-5
LCCN: 2016962149

10 9 8 7

Cover design by George Stevens.

This publication is designed to provide accurate and authoritative information in regard to the subject matter covered. It is sold with the understanding that the publisher is not engaged in rendering legal, accounting, or other professional services. If legal advice or other expert assistance is required, the services of a competent professional person should be sought.

Advantage Media Group is proud to be a part of the Tree Neutral® program. Tree Neutral offsets the number of trees consumed in the production and printing of this book by taking proactive steps such as planting trees in direct proportion to the number of trees used to print books. To learn more about Tree Neutral, please visit **www.treeneutral.com**.

Since 1917, the Forbes mission has remained constant. Global Champions of Entrepreneurial Capitalism. ForbesBooks exists to further that aim by bringing the Stories, Passion, and Knowledge of top thought leaders to the forefront. ForbesBooks brings you The Best in Business. To be considered for publication, please visit **www.forbesbooks.com**

To my amazing wife, Ivette—thank you for joining me on this incredible life's journey. I could not have done it without you! To my kids, Darien and Mason—thank you for making my life more meaningful.

Acknowledgments

This book would not be possible without the help and inspiration from the following people.

To my mother, Dora, and my father, Milton, thank you for the values you instilled in me that I still live by today. Dad, thank you for giving me my first job at twelve and for firing me so quickly. You, being an entrepreneur, inspired me to become one as well. Mom, I inherited your drive to never give up, to always do my best, and to be passionate about everything that I do.

To Jack Daly, my close friend, mentor, former business partner, and advisor. You have always inspired me to think bigger. Thank you for encouraging me to write this book. I truly enjoy living life to the fullest and sharing so many of those experiences with you.

To Jason Reid, you've put up with me through three businesses, and we are still the best of friends. Thank you for listening, for challenging my thinking, and for your continuous feedback to help make this book better.

To Brett Dillenberg, as cofounder at Platinum Capital, thank you for your loyalty, your friendship, your hard work every day, and for showing me how to have an honest and equitable partnership.

To my YPO forum-mates, Michael Maas, Ryan Rieches, David House, Terry Adams, Wil Smith, Josh McCarter, Andy Graham, and Jason Reid, your friendship and insights over the years have been invaluable. Much of your contributions have found their way onto these pages.

To Dawn Pope, thank you for always having my back, for making my work life easier, and for helping me free up the time and space to write this book. You are truly a pleasure to work with.

To my business coaches: Richard Carr, thank you for coaching me for over a decade, ensuring I knew my numbers and for teaching me to follow the five things it takes for a CEO to be successful. To Ron Ruther, you were my first advisor at twenty-four years old. Thank you for being so supportive and helpful. You were always there for me during both the good days and the bad. To Verne Harnish, thank you for creating the Birthing of Giants program and the Masters of Business Dynamics. Both taught me more about growing my business than anything else in life. To Vance Caesar, thank you for teaching me the coaching business and for helping me to focus on the clients that gave me energy and eliminate those who drained it. This alone helped me meaningfully raise my game.

To my coaching partners at CEO Coaching International: Jason Reid, Sheldon Harris, David Sobel, Michael Maas, and Steve Sanduski. Thank you for being such a strong group of leaders as we work together to enhance our best practices and improve the businesses and lives of entrepreneurs and CEOs around the world.

To my athletic coaches: Roch Frey, Ben Greenfield, and Lisa Komisza. Thank you for pushing me to achieve so much more than I could on my own.

To my clients, thank you for the privilege of coaching you and for allowing me to share your stories in this book. What I have learned from all of you is one of my greatest gifts.

To Steve Sanduski, thank you for taking an early draft of this book and reorganizing the concepts into a structure that is easy to follow and implement. I am truly grateful.

Finally, to my beautiful wife, Ivette, and our kids, Darien and Mason. Thank you for filling my life with purpose and joy.

Foreword

My relationship with Mark Moses began more than twenty years ago. At the time, I was delivering a two-and-a-half-day seminar on how to build a fast-growing and successful mortgage company. Mark was one of a hundred attendees. On the second day, he asked if he could take me to dinner. I could barely finish my meal as he pummeled me with questions. His energy was contagious, and his commitment to succeed was off the charts.

From there we began a multi-year consulting and training relationship. Eventually, I joined him as a third partner, and we had a highly successful seven-year run. I'm nearly a generation older than Mark, and when we first met he was a bachelor entrepreneur, neck deep in launching his new business. Today he is married and the proud dad to two great teenagers.

Along the way we both entered the triathlon sport, eventually competing at the Ironman level in races around the world. I've been honored to be included in the formal ceremonies in each of his children's Bar and Bat Mitzvahs. We've grown from business colleagues to dear friends.

All of the above history is to underscore that I know this man well. He walks his talk, whether it's business, sport, or family.

Building a business is hard work. Competing in the Ironman is hard work. Growing a loving, productive, and charitable family is hard work. Mark knows hard work. In my twenty-plus years in the speaking/training business, I've never seen a client that is as focused and able to knock off the list of things that matter most than Mark Moses.

The singular differentiator that Mark has possessed from the very start of our relationship is what I call Model the Masters. As our friendship grew, with a spread of fifteen years between us, I fully expected to have an influx of younger people entering my world. While there where certainly those in the employee ranks, when it came to the people closest to Mark in any advisory capacity, they tended to be my age or older.

Mark discovered early in life that those who had "been there, done that" could be his best teachers. His approach was to assertively seek out experienced input from mentors and coaches, thereby accelerating the growth of his business and his life.

He never went anywhere without his notepad and was always the curious one asking penetrating questions.

Beyond this inner circle of seasoned experience, Mark was regularly and actively doing a deep dive in a variety of learning forums: Entrepreneurs Organization (EO), Vistage, Young Presidents Organization (YPO), Birthing of Giants at MIT, Harvard Executive Learning Program, and Singularity University. He has spent his life leveraging the experiences of others in optimizing his performance in business, sport, and family. Again, he walks his talk.

What a natural transition in life for him to give birth to a CEO coaching business. And it's no surprise the company is delivering incredible results for its clients!

For several years, I encouraged Mark to "write the book" so he could share his expertise and make a positive impact on a much larger scale. *Make Big Happen!* is the result, and entrepreneurs and CEOs interested in how to live, work, and give BIG now have the guide. While the book is primarily focused on the business aspect of life, many of the concepts apply to one's personal life, too.

This is not an ivory tower book based on theory. *Make Big Happen!* is based on real world, proven, and practical application. Part of the magic of the book is its focus on the basics. Mark will challenge you through four questions.

1. ## What do you want?
2. ## What do you have to do?
3. ## What could get in the way?
4. ## How do you hold yourself accountable?

Mark is blunt, and he'll push you to up your game. It's the only way he knows to live.

You now have in your hands the playbook, the roadmap to success in your business and life. Now is the time to execute. Now is the time to *MAKE BIG HAPPEN!*

Jack Daly, CEO, Professional Sales Coach, Inc.
www.jackdaly.net

TABLE OF CONTENTS

Question 1: What Do You Want?

Question 2: What Do You Have to Do?

Question 3: What Could Get in the Way?

Question 4: How Do You Hold Yourself Accountable?

The 4 Qs to Make BIG Happen!

When I was seventeen, my dad declared bankruptcy. I had to grow up in a hurry.

Until then, life was good growing up in the small town of Sudbury, a mining community about 250 miles north of Toronto. My dad operated a retail men's clothing store. We were your typical middle-class family.

When I was twelve, Dad let me work in his store, selling suits to men. I soon became the top sales guy.

His regular staff wasn't exactly thrilled with how I was showing them up. So how did my dad respond to the staff's concern about this precocious young kid?

He fired me.

Dad said I caused too much drama and asked *too many questions.*

More than thirty years and several successful entrepreneurial ventures later, I am still asking questions.

As the founding partner of CEO Coaching International, a leading coaching organization for top entrepreneurs and CEOs, I have narrowed the questions down to just four. I call them The Make Big Happen Questions.

The Make Big Happen Questions is the most powerful tool I have found to cut to the heart of what makes people succeed in living, working, and giving.

When we engage clients in coaching, these questions frame our conversations and ensure we stay focused on what truly matters and what generates the results our clients desire.

1. What do you want? **(Vision)**

2. What do you have to do? **(Action)**

3. What could get in the way? **(Anticipate)**

4. How do you hold yourself accountable? **(Measure)**

You'll notice these questions apply not just in business but in all aspects of life.

IS THIS BOOK FOR YOU?

Make Big Happen! is not about accumulating the biggest toys or the most lavish house. It's not about jet-setting around the world on your private plane and staying in posh hotels.

Rather, it's about realizing you have locked inside you the potential to make life-changing things happen in how you live and support the ones you love, in how you express gratitude in giving back, and in how you build businesses that exceed the needs of your clients.

A wonderful standard of living is often the outcome, but it is not the objective.

When I wrote this book, I was very clear about whom I was trying to reach.

> *If you're an entrepreneur or CEO who's tired of less-than-stellar results or who knows you're sitting on a goldmine but haven't been able to maximize your results, then this book is for you. If you have dreamed about starting your own business, this book may inspire you to take the next step.*

My dad's bankruptcy was just the first of several life-shaping traumas that helped to clarify my thinking and guide me over the past three decades.

A severe family health challenge, a disloyal business partner, uncontrollable economic changes—I've been through them all and more. And through my experiences, I've realized The Make Big Happen Questions are a magic elixir of sorts.

They kept me focused on what truly mattered in the way I live, the way I build my businesses, and the way I give back.

Make Big Happen! is a guide to help you answer these questions for your own unique situation so you can live, work, and give BIG!

The questions are universal, and the impact is immense.

Throughout the book, I share specific examples of how these questions are used by entrepreneurs and CEOs all over the world to make dramatic improvements in their businesses and lives.

Like you, I am tired of books that are long on theory but short on real world, practical examples of how to implement what is discussed. Not here.

My clients gave the green light to share their stories and the results they generated by following through on these questions. And, of course, I weave my own experiences throughout.

So if you are ready to *make BIG happen* in your life and in your business, read on.

HOW THIS BOOK IS ORGANIZED

Make Big Happen! is divided into four sections based on The Make Big Happen Questions. I recommend you read the book sequentially, as the questions make the most sense when read in the context of this order.

1. WHAT DO YOU WANT? (VISION)

It all starts here. You have to know with great certainty what you want.

Without this clarity, the circumstances of life will determine your results, instead of you grabbing the proverbial bull by the horns and intentionally living, working, and giving the way you want, with whom you want, and where you want.

With clarity, you'll get the results you specifically desire. And years from now, when you look back over the course of your life, you will say, "Well done."

2. WHAT DO YOU HAVE TO DO? (ACTION)

Knowing what you want is critical. It points you in the right direction.

This second question is all about identifying the specific activities you need to implement on a consistent basis to generate what you said you want.

It's like the laws of physics. Implementing a certain activity will lead to a predictable result.

I'll share examples of the specific activities entrepreneurs and CEOs around the world are implementing to build businesses that are life changing for both themselves and their clients.

3. WHAT COULD GET IN THE WAY? (ANTICIPATE)

You know as well as I do, things don't always go as planned. Yet, with a few simple strategies, you can overcome many of the potential pitfalls that derail lesser entrepreneurs and CEOs than you.

I learned this the hard way.

I saw it in my dad's clothing business. I experienced it in running my own multimillion-dollar businesses. Now, I coach clients on how to overcome and plan for the foreseeable setbacks and use these threats to build even more rock-solid businesses.

4. HOW DO YOU HOLD YOURSELF
ACCOUNTABLE? (MEASURE)

I run a coaching company, so you may think this is self-serving. I get it.

But here's the deal. You need accountability, whether it is through my organization or somewhere else.

My broader mission is to empower entrepreneurs and CEOs around the world to build life-changing businesses and live exemplary lives. Accountability is the final piece required to ensure it happens.

This section is about putting accountability systems in place so you have the support, the tough love, and the camaraderie of fellow leaders who are on a similar journey.

MAKE BIG HAPPEN!

When you follow the process above and add burning desire to the mix, you'll be unstoppable. It has worked for me.

I am 5'4" tall. I've been height-challenged all my life. But what I lack in height, I make up in heart.

I have built and sold businesses that generated hundreds of millions of dollars in revenue. I'm an Ernst & Young's Entrepreneur of the Year award winner and won the Blue Chip Enterprise award for overcoming adversity.

After winning the US National Squash Championship.

On the sports side, I have completed twelve full-distance Ironman Triathlons, including five Hawaii Ironmans, and I'm a US National Squash Champion.

On the personal side, my family has overcome health scares that have torn other families apart. We've made it a point to spend quality time together, and we've been blessed to have traveled the world.

On giving back, I've raised substantial money for charities and sat on numerous charitable boards.

I don't share this to brag. I simply want you to know that if a short kid from a small town in Canada can *make BIG happen*, so can you.

Finishing the Hawaii Ironman.

Read the book. Implement the principles. And you'll *make BIG happen* in your life.

I look forward to sharing the journey with you.

QUESTION 1

what do you **want**?

Proceed with Vision

"This painting thing, it's crazy. That'll never work," my dad said to me when he first heard about my business pursuit.

At the time, I had just started college and was trying to figure out how I was going to pay for tuition the next fall. My part-time lifeguarding gig was nice, but it wouldn't pay all the bills.

One day, at the college career center, I saw a sign: "Be your own boss," it said. "You can earn $5,000 to $15,000 in a summer by having your own Student Painter franchise."

I figured that sounded like me. Student Painters was a remarkable concept. It taught college students how to run their own businesses.

The students who participated were in the business of painting houses, but it was not house painting they were most interested in learning. They were there to learn about business.

Left: Fueling up en route to the United States.
Right: Mark's Student Painters business was a booming success.

They wanted to learn how to be entrepreneurs. They wanted to know how to build a business, handle money and payroll, market and sell services, deal with customers, interview and hire people, and learn how to deal with adversity and challenges.

I applied and got the job. I opened a new territory in Waterloo, Ontario, my college town, and that first summer, I was the top rookie franchisee in Canada and made $18,000, while my entire college expenses were $4,000. "This entrepreneur stuff is pretty cool," I said to myself. I had expected to be studying accounting in college. It wasn't long before I started to think that I could be the guy who hired the accountant.

I did it again the following summer. But, this time I was the International Franchisee of the Year. I was twenty years old and earned $35,000 that summer.

At that point, I knew I had to run my own business, so I convinced the franchise company to partner with me. It didn't take long before I packed up my U-Haul and drove south to the United States to launch the business.

As I was packing, my dad told me: "You will be back. That'll never work."

I took his comment as a challenge. It drove me to win. Despite the long odds—after all, I was a startup in a foreign country—I was determined to succeed. I didn't want to face the music if I failed.

Eventually, I ended up in California and opened my Student Painters business.

I went from zero to 250 branches, employing more than three thousand students by my fourth year in business.

Looking back, my initial vision was simply to make enough money to pay for college. Over time, the vision grew as I realized the vastness of the world's opportunities.

Through it all, a clear vision of what I was trying to accomplish was the key.

Recruiting for his Student Painters business.

CEOs often lack this clarity of vision. Yes, they have an idea of what they want, but they don't have laser-like focus. Vision plus focus plus emotional intensity enables you to accomplish great things.

SET VISION FROM THE TOP

It's the responsibility of the leader of the company to set the vision, to communicate it, and to embed it into the culture of the organization.

True vision inspires greatness and helps *make BIG happen!* Think of how many people Nike inspired with "Just do it." Or how rapidly Google has grown with its vision to organize all of the data in the world and make it accessible for everyone in a useful way.

The point is this: If you know where you are going, you have a much higher probability of getting there.

It is a cliché, but it is very true: the leaders of the firm have to work *on* the business, not in the business.

Too many leaders get caught up in the whirlwind of the day at the expense of focusing on what's truly important—*getting to where they want to go.* The CEOs who truly perform are the ones who spend significant time, at a high level, executing the vision. They begin with the end in mind, working the plan backward.

Apple is the poster child for laser-like focus in regard to their vision.

In a 2012 *Harvard Business Review* article, Walter Isaacson, author of the definitive Steve Jobs biography, described how

Jobs became maniacal about focusing the company on its key opportunities:

When Jobs returned to Apple in 1997, it was producing a random array of computers and peripherals, including a dozen different versions of the Macintosh. After a few weeks of product review sessions, he'd finally had enough. "Stop!" he shouted. "This is crazy." He grabbed a Magic Marker, padded in his bare feet to a whiteboard, and drew a two-by-two grid. "Here's what we need," he declared. Atop the two columns, he wrote "Consumer" and "Pro." He labeled the two rows "Desktop" and "Portable." Their job, he told his team members, was to focus on four great products, one for each quadrant. All other products should be canceled. There was a stunned silence. But by getting Apple to focus on making just four computers, he saved the company. "Deciding what not to do is as important as deciding what to do," he told me. "That's true for companies, and it's true for products."

Apple is all about making insanely great products.

Tim Cook, who succeeded Jobs after his untimely death, continues this tradition and said, "We believe in saying no to thousands of projects, so that we can really focus on the few that are truly important and meaningful to us."

The vision at Apple is clearly outliving its founder—a sign of an enduring ideal.

Consider the example of Michael Phelps, who went to the Olympics with one goal in mind: to win eight gold medals. Why eight? Because Mark Spitz had seven, and Phelps wanted to set the world record.

But Phelps didn't just show up, take a few warm up laps, and expect to rock and roll. He followed years of protocol to prepare himself for this event. He envisioned winning those eight medals, and he positioned himself to qualify for the right competitions.

In short, Phelps was like other winners in that he focused on the important, not the urgent. His strategy was "ready, aim, fire." Far too many people approach life and business as "ready, fire, aim."

The typical CEO probably makes only three or four decisions per year that really matter. True, they are called upon to make decisions every day—but do those decisions move the ball? What matters are the big, strategic decisions—the relatively rare ones that chart a company's course and that fulfill its vision.

It's these decisions that you—as the CEO—should devote your energy to.

COMMUNICATE, COMMUNICATE, COMMUNICATE

Vision also requires good communication. Verne Harnish calls it "having a good rhythm." As a graduate of Verne's "Birthing of Giants" program, I have been an advocate of his Rockefeller Habits program for years.

It's important to have an ongoing systematic communication process throughout the year to keep the entire team updated on company progress, and it reinforces the culture you desire.

Here is an outline of a communication calendar I've used successfully for many years.

➡ Annually

State of the Company address. Share where your company is going and what it will take to get there. Review the past year, recognize those who made a difference, and get everyone revved up for the coming year. Open up for questions, and be very transparent.

➡ Quarterly

Planning session with leadership team. Here is where you ask tough questions and are brutally honest with your answers.

- What went right this quarter?
- What went wrong?
- What have we learned?
- Did we do what we said we would do?
- Where did we miss, and why?
- What are the biggest opportunities that have come up this quarter?
- What are the biggest challenges, and how are we dealing with them?
- What new goals should we set for the quarter, and how can we ensure they are aligned with our annual plan?

➔ Monthly

Leadership team update to its staff. This is the perfect time to mix business updates with employee recognition.

- Share how the company did compared with how it expected to do, and then talk about what went right and wrong.

- Share your plans for the coming quarter, and discuss what initiatives will be pursued.

- Recognize people who made a difference.

- Celebrate service anniversaries and birthdays.

- Introduce the new people.

Company video or newsletter. The CEO should send a personalized monthly communication to all staff and use it to inspire the team and reinforce the team's engagement to the company.

➔ Weekly

Working session with leadership team. Discuss and review progress on initiatives and who might need help from whom to make things happen. Keep the focus on strategic initiatives identified at the quarterly meeting as most important in achieving the company's goals, not the urgent issue of the day.

➔ Daily

Huddle with each management team. This can be a 10-15 minute huddle of the management team, the sales team, the operations team, the customer service team, or whomever. The leader of the group calls the members together to touch base, discuss any urgent issues, and clear the deck so everybody can go about their day without frequent interruptions.

If there is one universal complaint among employees around the world, it is this: a lack of communication from the boss. Don't be that boss. Communicate freely and frequently. Share your dream and vision. Create alignment to that vision and get your people to buy in. You'll be surprised how many people want to go along for the ride.

VISION VERSUS MISSION

So far, I have talked about the vision—about how having a vision gives you clarity for running the business and how you can nurture it through communication.

But what about the company's mission statement?

I think of a company vision as the "what" and the company mission as the "why."

The vision is inspirational and aspirational. It's what your company will look like if you have hit all your goals and dreams. It should challenge and inspire your employees.

The mission is why you exist. It supports the vision and helps guide stakeholders in living the company's purpose and direction. It answers the "why" you exist by describing what your company does, whom it does it for, and how it does what it does.

To use a mountain-climbing metaphor, the mission is why and how you are climbing the mountain. The vision is the view when you are standing on the summit.

Each has their place within a company. I place a heavy focus on the vision and recommend you start here because everything emanates from answering this initial question, "What do you want." If you don't start there, you'll wander aimlessly and lack the disciplined focus necessary to thrive in a competitive business environment.

Once you have your vision in place, you can turn your attention to your mission.

The following template is a good outline to follow when developing your mission.

> Our mission is to _____ *(do what)*, for _____ *(whom are you doing it for)* by _____ *(how do you do it)* so _____ *(why you do it)*.

Here's a simple example based on the above template.

> *ABC Company's mission is to remove the roadblocks to investing for all investors by creating an easy-to-use technology platform with low account minimums so every person can reach financial freedom.*

Getting clarity on your vision and mission is not something that will happen in one meeting. I encourage leaders to set aside quality time to discuss these critical company guideposts. It often helps to leave the office and go on an executive retreat so you can work on this free from the whirlwind of distractions.

Once completed, your vision and mission should become part of the fabric of your organization. It should permeate all you do and guide you in your decision-making process.

You'll know the vision and mission are embedded in your culture when you're able to stop any employee in the hallway and listen to them share your firm's vision and mission with enthusiasm and pride.

You should communicate it freely and frequently both inside and outside the company.

Vision and mission statements are much more than just words. Done well, they can set your company on a path to greatness.

Chapter 1 Action Steps

☑ Develop a compelling vision for your company's future.

☑ Develop a mission for your company to give further direction to all your stakeholders.

☑ Communicate your vision and mission throughout the company.

☑ Use your vision and mission to help create a thriving corporate culture.

☑ Implement a regular cadence of accountability and planning meetings including daily, weekly, monthly, quarterly, and annual.

CHAPTER 2

Determine Your Huge Outrageous Targets (HOTs)

The world is full of business opportunities. There's certainly no lack of things we could do. But that is also the problem. How do we choose what to work on from among the endless options?

Years ago, my colleague and good friend Jack Daly and I sat down for a talk after a particularly rough stretch at our company, Platinum Capital. We needed a way to rally our team, to come up with something that would energize them after the tough time we were all going through.

We came up with what we called a Huge Outrageous Target (HOT). It was a goal so big and so outrageous that it sparked a fire in our team and gave them a way forward to new growth.

Over the years, we have refined the concept, and now it is an integral part of how our client companies *Make Big Happen!*

Jack Daly and Mark Moses

A HOT is the one goal (or at most, two) that matters most. It gives direction to the firm, and failure to achieve it will make every other accomplishment pale by comparison.

As entrepreneurs and CEOs, it's difficult to set HOTs because we always want to do more. We're drawn to the next shiny object. We get antsy and have ADD.

The discipline of setting HOTs keeps us in check and focused on the absolute-most-critical goal for our company.

How do you determine a HOT for your company?

The key is to look for leverage. Ask yourself, "What HOT, when achieved, would have the greatest impact on our business?" You are looking for a HOT that will deliver outsized impact on your business and perhaps even help your company grow exponentially.

Properly set, your HOT should inspire, motivate, reinforce your vision, and drive your culture of performance.

Here are several points to consider when setting HOTs:

1.   Have an overarching HOT for the company as a whole.

2.   Teams or business units should focus on no more than two HOTs at the same time.

3.   The battles you choose must win the war.

4.   Senior leaders can veto but not dictate.

5.   All HOTs must have a finish line in the form of "from X to Y by Z" (what to what by when).

Depending on the size of your company, you may have multiple HOTs throughout the organization. Think of it in terms of a war.

The "big HOT" comes from the top. It's the war. It's the most important overriding HOT at the company, and the leadership team is responsible for setting it, with input from appropriate stakeholders.

Below the war are battles, and each battle leads to eventually winning the war. Lower levels of the organization can set their own HOTs, but they must be designed to help achieve success of the higher HOTs and win the "war."

WORK YOUR HOTS

I am a big fan of the book *The Four Disciplines of Execution: Achieving Your Wildly Important Goals* by McChesney, Covey, and Huling at the FranklinCovey organization. The authors do a nice job of describing how to execute on your big goals—what they call "wildly important goals."

Similarly, when I speak to entrepreneurial audiences around the world, I often ask them if they can produce a one-page plan for the coming year complete with what is going to guarantee they can get it done. Unfortunately, 90 percent of them cannot.

These are not small mom-and-pop shops; they are businesses with revenues that range between $5 million and $50 million, some even meaningfully larger. They really struggle with the "what is it going to take that is specific and measurable to guarantee we get it done."

So where do you want to be twelve months from now? What do you desire in terms of growing your company's revenues and profits? And what's going to guarantee that you get there?

Once you know where you are going, the key is to identify those HOTs and then determine the specific and measurable activities that your company should undertake that will lead to those outcomes.

In line with what McChesney, Covey, and Huling suggest, these should be leading activities, not lag measures. A lag measure is the measurement of the goal. It is based on what has already happened.

By contrast, leading activities foretell the result. They are predictive in that executing on the leading activities will foretell changes in lag measures.

As you develop your HOTs and determine your leading activities, you must vet your plan with your coach, trusted advisors, or colleagues to ensure you are in fact starting with the right strategies. Then, make it a priority for you and your leadership team to spend the majority of your time working on the leading activities that will lead to the desired results.

A breakdown most often occurs when the leadership team is trying to establish the HOTs and connect them to the specific leading activities. The key is to make sure you pick the right leading activities. You have to be certain that executing the leading activities are truly the drivers that will lead to achieving your HOT. We'll discuss this further in chapter 5.

After setting the HOTs and determining the leading activities, you must follow through with developing a scoreboard. Similar to a sporting event, your scoreboard should track your progress toward achieving your HOTs and be easily accessible to everybody in your organization.

How do you ensure people follow through on the HOTs? It's called accountability. Whether you hire a coach or each team member holds each other responsible for following through, you need an accountability system.

One simple accountability system is to hold a weekly meeting with your team, as I discussed in chapter 1. At this meeting, each member reports on what they committed to do that week, the scoreboard is reviewed, and new commitments are made for the next week. This is the process I follow with my coaching clients to keep them focused on their HOTs.

This system of setting HOTs, developing leading activities, using a scoreboard to track lagging indicators, and practicing accountability is not just theory. It works in the real world.

For example, my client Sheldon Wolitski, CEO of The Select Group in Raleigh, NC, decided to follow this methodology and grew his company from $18 million to over $100 million over the last five years. More importantly, the company grew its gross margin from 24 to 30 percent.

My good friend and colleague David Sobel was masterful at tracking and executing the leading sales activities that led to a very meaningful liquidity event for their firm, Home Warranty of America. During the process to sell the company, due diligence went on for much longer than expected, but David led his team to stay clearly focused on the leading activities. And as a result of his relentless focus, the company beat the plan every month during due diligence.

Bill Keen distinctly remembers when he was ten years old, sitting on his father's couch in his apartment, waiting for the unemployment check to hit the mailbox. He could see the anxiety in his father's eyes. And at that young age, Bill started to understand how important financial security is to having peace of mind.

Perhaps not surprisingly, Bill went to college, studied finance, and became one of the country's top financial advisors through his firm, Keen Wealth Advisors, in Overland Park, Kansas.

Bill's firm has experienced tremendous growth. His desire to achieve financial security for his clients clearly permeates his desire to achieve top results for his firm, too.

Recently, Bill's team achieved their annual goal in terms of new qualified prospects by the end of the first quarter. How did they do it? They kept score.

The team just kept beating the daily and weekly goal, and by the end of the quarter they had achieved their HOT. Bill said the impact of focusing on the leading activity has him on track to well surpass his HOT of net assets under management.

If your organization lacks a HOT, put the wheels in motion now to develop one. Nothing else matters if you do not have a clear understanding of your company's most important goals.

Chapter 2 Action Steps

☑ Think about what would have to happen in your company in order for it to become transformed into something you can only dream about today.

☑ Develop one or two Huge Outrageous Targets (HOTs) that, when met, will transform your company into that dream.

☑ Depending on your company size, develop one or two HOTs at the departmental level.

CHAPTER 3

Ignite Your Passion

Are you living your life by design or by chance? Are you living the life you truly want? Or are you hitting the snooze bar so you can get a few extra minutes of sleep?

If you're hitting the snooze bar, think of it as your wake-up call. Now is the time to make changes so you'll go to bed at night looking forward to getting up the next morning.

Let's face it, as entrepreneurs and CEOs, separating our business from our personal life just doesn't happen. We cannot be happy in one area and miserable in the other and expect the "happy one" to be unaffected. It just doesn't work that way.

The most successful entrepreneurs and CEOs have found ways to seamlessly live the life Virgin's Richard Branson described when he said, "I don't think of work as work and play as play, it's all living." They have a vision that encompasses their entire life, not just their work.

PREEMPT THE REGRETS

Bronnie Ware was a palliative nurse for many years, and she spent her time sitting with people for three to twelve weeks as they prepared to die. She often asked them about any regrets they had or anything they would do differently and noticed several common things came up over and over. Here are the top five as she wrote in a *Huffington Post* article.

1. They wish they'd had the courage to live a life true to themselves, not a life that others expected of them.

2. They wish they hadn't worked so hard.

3. They wish they'd had the courage to express their feelings.

4. They wish they had stayed in touch with friends.

5. They wish they had let themselves be happier.

Looking at the list, these are all things each of us can get better at every day.

When I was forty, I participated in a fascinating exercise with my forum at the Young Presidents Organization. We were nine CEOs running companies. Each of us was asked to prepare his eightieth birthday speech and then deliver it to the others.

The exercise is a look into the future, and yet it incorporates elements of the past. Much of it involves relationships: with a spouse, with siblings, with parents. We were young men imagining ourselves as old men:

Mark with fellow members of the Young Presidents Organization.

➔ How successful had we become?

➔ How successful were our children?

➔ Had we stayed fit?

➔ What was the state of our spirituality?

➔ Did we do well in marriage?

➔ What kind of friendships had we developed?

➔ At eighty, were we living the lives that we had aspired to live when we were forty?

Man, those were some tough questions to answer. How would you answer them?

Our lives are filled with choices: where we live and work, what we do, whom we marry, the friends we choose, the religion we practice, whether we will stay fit.

We can choose to eliminate from our lives the things that drain us and, instead, spend our time on the pursuits that give us energy and ignite our passions for our work and life.

By being intentional about our choices and having meaningful conversations with our loved ones, we can avoid the deathbed regrets that Bronnie Ware so painfully encountered.

MAKE A COMMITMENT

Once we decide on our direction, an important element for success is commitment. We need to be committed to what we want to do—despite what others tell us and despite the naysayers around us.

Setting annual, three-year, five-year, and ten-year goals is a great way to turn your commitments into measurable outcomes.

I've been setting annual goals since my late teens. Back then, I set a goal to be a millionaire by the time I was thirty. I achieved it by age twenty-six. I wrote down that I wanted to win the US squash championships by the time I was thirty, and I met that goal two years early. Later on, I set a goal to complete an Ironman Triathlon in under thirteen hours. I checked that one off when I finished my first Ironman in twelve hours and fifty-five minutes.

Thousands of books have been written on goal setting, so we do not need to rehash it here. The key point is you have to have a game plan for how you are going to make your dreams and

Mark and his wife, Ivette, after completing an Ironman Triathlon in Hawaii.

aspirations come true. You have to be focused and disciplined in pursuing your plan. Setting goals allows you to track your progress along the way.

Think about the people who appear on the television show *The Biggest Loser*. They have finally committed to losing weight— and sometimes are able to drop well over a hundred pounds. They failed in the past, but this time they succeed. This time they have committed to a disciplined plan.

Sister Madonna Buder, at age eighty-four, is still competing in Ironman triathlons. She's a legend. She does it because she can, and it makes her feel good. She is focused, disciplined, and living her life by design, not by chance. How many nuns are out there competing in Ironman? How many are doing it in their eighties?

Mark and his daughter, Darien.

Rick and Dick Hoyt are another Ironman inspiration. The father pushes his son, who is now in his forties, in a wheelchair. They have completed many marathons and triathlons, including the Hawaiian Ironman.

My daughter Darien is a great example of the power of making a commitment. For years, she was a competitive gymnast who worked out several hours a day. And let me tell you, the strength exercises she had to do made me, as an Ironman competitor, wince. It paid off. She regularly stood on top of the podium, including winning the California State Championship.

A few years ago, I sat with a table full of CEOs who had traveled in for Ironman California 70.3 in San Diego. They were all talking nonsense about who was going to place first. Instead of chiming in with my normal bravado, I was moaning about an injury I was nursing.

In steps Darien.

She was twelve at the time and said, "Dad, stop talking about it, just do it!" That shut me right up. The next day I kicked all their asses. She gave me a memento that sits on my desk with that message as a reminder. Darien taught me an important lesson that day about the power of commitment.

Like the contestants on *The Biggest Loser*, Sister Madonna Buder, Rick and Dick Hoyt, and my daughter Darien, you need to stay committed to your vision and to your goals in order to live the life you desire.

Staying true to your commitments also means there are times when you must say no. Most of us want to say yes whenever we are asked for a few minutes of our time, whether it is to join a board or attend a certain party. But if you are truly ready to live the life you desire, then there are times when you have to say no to the request. Be protective of your time, and save your yes for the activities you enjoy, are passionate about, and are meaningful to you and your loved ones.

DON'T BE THE SMARTEST PERSON IN THE ROOM

On your life journey, consider the nature of your friendships. As Jim Rohn said, "You are the average of the five people you spend the most time with." If you hang out with winners, you will likely be a winner, too. It's no surprise that Warren Buffett hangs out with Bill Gates. On the other hand, if you hang out with losers, you will likely be a loser, too.

I see it so often when I go into schools to speak to kids. It is clear to me who will be the winners. By the time they get into high school, young people are already choosing their direction. Those who spend their time with losers will fall under their influence and move down that sad path. Those who choose to associate with winners are on their way to victories.

As the old saying goes, if you're the smartest person in the room, it's time to find a new room.

START A BUCKET LIST

Do you have a bucket list? As you may recall, Jack Nicholson and Morgan Freeman starred in the movie *The Bucket List* as two men facing death who set out to experience their lifelong dreams before "kicking the bucket."

If you haven't started your list, it's as simple as taking out a piece of paper and writing down the things you would like to do in the years to come. Be creative. Having a bucket list and "checking them off" is a great way to keep the snooze bar at bay.

I share my bucket list with my friends, and the ensuing conversation is motivating for all of us.

Here are a few of the things on my bucket list of 167 items. Many of them have been checked off, and I keep adding to the list. Maybe they will spark some ideas for you:

- ☑ Land on an aircraft carrier.
- ☑ Ride in the Goodyear blimp.
- ☑ Climb a fourteen-thousand-foot mountain.
- ☐ Climb Mt. Kilimanjaro.
- ☐ Eat breakfast at Mount Everest base camp.
- ☑ Take yearly one-on-one trips with my two children.

Clockwise from Top: Mark and his wife, Ivette, cycling through Italy. At the summit of Mt. Whitney with friends Michael Maas and Terry Adams. Mark during the Great Wall Marathon. With his son, Jason, at the Ice Hotel in Quebec City.

☑ Cycle with my wife through Tuscany (also completed Provence; Puglia, Italy; Napa/Sonoma; Burgundy).

☐ Cycle with my kids in different countries around the world.

☑ Spend a month in Europe with my family. (Done three times.)

☑ Go on an African safari with my wife.

☑ Ring the bell at a stock exchange (Nasdaq 2013).

☑ Complete the Great Wall Marathon.

☐ Complete an Ironman triathlon on each continent. (I have two left: Asia and Africa.)

☐ Complete a marathon in every continent. (I have one left: Africa.)

☐ Complete the North Pole Marathon (scheduled for October 2016).

☑ Complete the Antarctica Marathon.

☐ Visit a hundred countries (currently at sixty-nine).

☐ Complete the Grand Canyon Rim-to-Rim-to-Rim (scheduled for September 2016).

☐ Visit Machu Picchu.

Related to my bucket list, I've even designed how life will look when my wife and I are empty nesters. We have already resolved to go off by ourselves for regular vacations throughout the year. We plan to live four months a year in Europe, which we love, continue our cycling trips together in exotic locales, and pursue our passion to visit one hundred countries. As we look to the years ahead, we know we must be constantly comparing notes on our individual bucket lists so we can make the most of the time we have been given together.

Mark with his son, Mason, and Jack Daly
at the Antarctica marathon.

As you can see, my bucket list is diverse, and I've been blessed to put a checkmark by many of the items and continue to make solid progress on others. The beauty of a bucket list is that you are being intentional about what you want to do in life. You are laying out a path to *Make Big Happen.*

"STAY HUNGRY, STAY FOOLISH"

Steve Jobs delivered a memorable commencement address at Stanford University on June 12, 2005. Here's an excerpt that fits right in with the idea of living your life by design and without regrets:

> *Sometimes life can hit you in the head with a brick. Don't lose faith. I'm convinced that the only thing that kept me going was that I loved what I did. You've got to find what*

you love. And that is as true for your work as it is for your lovers. There is no reason not to follow your heart.

Your work is going to fill a large part of your life, and the only way to be truly satisfied is to do what you believe is great work—and the only way to do great work is to love what you do. If you haven't found it yet, keep looking, and don't settle.

Don't let the noise of other's opinions drown out your inner voice. And most important, have the courage to follow your heart and intuition. They somehow already know what you truly want to find.

Stay hungry. Stay foolish.

Take the time to read the full address at http://news.stanford.edu/news/2005/june15/jobs-061505.html. It's a good use of your time.

BE LIKE THE WISE FISHERMAN

To illustrate the importance of building the life you want, let me share an old tale of a Mexican fisherman. I do not know where the story originated—it has been around for a long time—but it perfectly captures the perspective that I wish to leave you with in this chapter:

In a small, coastal village in Mexico, a businessman was down at the pier watching a small fishing boat approach. When the fisherman docked, the businessman noticed several large tuna in the boat. The businessman com-

plimented the fisherman on the quality of his catch and asked him how long it had taken him to catch them.

"Only a little while," the fisherman said.

"If you had stayed out longer, you could have caught more such fish!" the businessman said.

"Yes, but this will be enough for my family and me," the fisherman responded.

"What do you do with the rest of your time?"

"I sleep late, fish a little, play with my children, take a siesta with my wife, Maria, and then each evening I stroll into the village where I sip wine and play guitar with my amigos," the fisherman said. "I have a full and busy life, señor."

The businessman scoffed. "I am a Harvard MBA," he said. "I can help you. This is what you should do. You should spend more of your time fishing and make more money so that you can buy a bigger boat. With a bigger boat, you soon will make enough money to buy several boats. Eventually, you will have a fleet of fishing boats. You will not have to sell your catch to a middleman—you will be able to sell directly to a processor, and eventually you can open your own cannery. You will control the product, processing, and distribution. You will be able to leave this fishing village and move to Mexico City—and then on to Los Angeles and to New York City, where you can run your expanding enterprise."

"Señor, how long will this all take?"

"Fifteen or twenty years," the businessman replied.

"But what then, señor?"

The businessman laughed and said, "That's the best part! When the time is right, you can announce an IPO and sell your company stock to the public and become very rich. You could make millions."

"Millions, señor? Then what?"

"Then you can retire. You can move to a small coastal fishing village where you can sleep late, fish a little, play with your kids, take a siesta with your wife, and stroll to the village in the evenings to sip wine and play your guitar with your amigos."

The fisherman looked at him and smiled.

ASSESS THE LIFE YOU'RE LIVING

In both my coaching practice and group presentations, I use a workbook that includes a valuable self-assessment for determining whether you are living the life you want. I ask participants to break their self-assessment into eight categories, which collectively we refer to as the "Wheel of Life." Those categories are health, business/career, family, spiritual, ability to say no, energy, life, and friends.

The participants rate how they are doing on each of those categories based on these prompt questions:

> ➲ Do you feel you are taking care of your health with a good diet and sufficient sleep?

- How do you feel about your business or career—are you passionate about it?

- What is the state of your family relationships, particularly spouse and children?

- How do you view your spiritual development, and how might you improve it?

- Have you learned to say no, and how often do you say yes when you mean no?

- Are you doing the things that increase your energy or deplete it?

- Are you living the life you want?

- Do you have the friends you want, and are you spending enough time with them?

Participants rate each consideration on a scale of one to ten, and then they ponder how they could improve each rating to get closer to a ten.

Finally, I ask participants to create their bucket list. I ask them to have their significant other create one, too. Once both are completed, you should combine the lists and put proposed dates on the calendar to achieve your goals. You may find that your bucket list differs from that of your significant other. This is a great opportunity for the two of you to start talking so life doesn't pass you by before you begin to achieve your dreams.

If you are not living your life by design, ask why not? What is holding you back?

Take the time to figure out what you want. Start writing down some ideas. Determine how your work and play seamlessly coexist. Create a bucket list.

Many people are already living the life they designed. You can too.

Chapter 3 Action Steps

☑ Make the decision and commit to achieving what you set out to do; don't let the naysayers get in the way.

☑ Start a bucket list and make plans to systematically knock them off the list.

☑ Complete the self-assessment, and start redesigning your life to match what is ideal for you and your family.

NEXT QUESTION

Once you figure out what you want, the next step is to identify the specific activities you need to do to guarantee you get it. And that leads us to Question 2.

QUESTION 2

what do you **have** to do

Focus on the Five Important Things

In working with CEOs who want to build high-growth companies, I have repeatedly seen the same characteristics of effective leadership—across industries, across countries, across continents. The CEOs whom I know to be truly top performers always seem to focus on five things.

> 1. **Vision.** The CEO is responsible for the vision of the company. They should drive the answer to the question, "Where are we going?" It is a question that calls for clarity, painstaking communication, and dedication to aligning your company culture to your vision.

> 2. **Cash.** At the end of the day, the CEO is ultimately responsible to ensure the company has enough cash to achieve its plans. The CEO should be thoroughly aware of the numbers, the key indicators, and should review

monthly cash flow statements, a daily cash report, and a monthly projection.

3. People. The CEO's job is to ensure we have the right people in the right jobs. Creating an environment that will attract the kind of talent needed to pursue and execute on the vision is also critical.

4. Key Relationships. The CEO is ultimately responsible for the key relationships in the company. Key relationships are the ones that matter most and would be a big blow to the company if they went away.

5. Learning. CEOs must continue to sharpen their game. They should devote time to the pursuit of learning what is happening in their industry and related industries. We live in a world of wonders in which innovations come so fast that it is hard to keep up. But we must keep up. For businesses, it's a matter of survival.

If you dream of taking your company to $100 million or more, if you want to move the puck down the ice, these are the five crucial elements on which you as the CEO must focus.

In Question 1, I discussed the importance of vision and the benefits of having clarity in business and in life. Now, let's take a look at the four other areas where CEOs should spend their time.

CASH: KNOW YOUR NUMBERS

I've been around high-growth companies for decades. I have spent years building and coaching high-growth companies. And I know that when a company is growing quickly, it faces an incredible drain on cash. So one of the first things you should do is make sure you have a handle on your cash situation.

Remember, profit does not equal cash. Accounts receivable do not equal cash. Inventory does not equal cash. Cash equals cash, plain and simple.

You could grow really fast and make a lot of profit but run out of cash. When you run out of cash, you're out of business.

I've also learned that while cash solves problems, a lack of it creates them. The dilemma is that as a company grows and invests in people, equipment, space, etc., it eats cash. So how is it possible that a thriving business can be making a profit but lack cash flow? It's because you invest a dollar today to grow the business, but you don't get that dollar back in "cash in the bank" for sixty days. You can "grow broke" in those sixty days.

In turbulent times, the challenge isn't whether you will get paid within thirty days but rather whether it might take ninety days if something goes sideways with a client. Or worse, the client might not pay you at all. Now your business is in jeopardy. While you are waiting to get paid, you still need to cover expenses. So the lesson in good times and bad is that cash is not cash until it is cash. Your P&L may show profit, but if it is tied up in accounts receivable or inventory, you have a problem.

Here are five keys to managing your cash so you don't "grow broke":

1.   Review your daily cash position.

That's right, take a look at your cash in the bank daily. Look at the trend; is it growing, shrinking, or staying the same? Compare it to accounts receivable and accounts payable. If accounts receivable are growing faster than your cash, you have a problem brewing.

2.   Shorten your cash-operating cycle.

Every firm needs to calculate its cash-operating cycle. It measures the time from when the money leaves your business to the time you get it back in the form of cash in the bank. Take a look at the diagram:

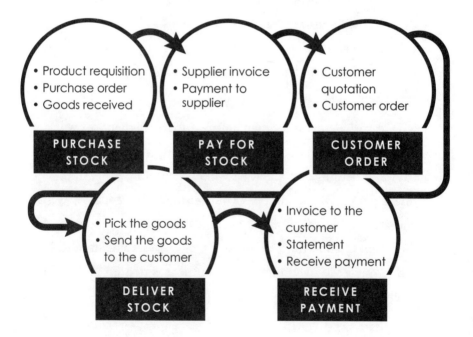

All the way on the left is the time when you take the inventory on. Following the arrow, next you pay for the inventory. Then you get to the point where you actually sell that inventory. Finally, at some time out on the right side of the diagram, you get paid. That is the cash-operating cycle, and most firms have no idea what theirs is. Even in a service business, this cycle exists, minus the inventory portion.

Keep in mind, the more you can decrease your cash-operating cycle, the more cash you create. The more cash you create, the faster you can grow. The best article I've seen written on this topic was in the *Harvard Business Review*. It's called "How Fast Can Your Company Afford to Grow?" by Neil Churchill and John Mullins. It's a short read, but I cannot imagine running a business without a grasp on those concepts.

Here are five ways to shorten your cash-operating cycle:

1. Ask your clients to pay you more quickly. If you give them thirty days to pay, make it fifteen. If you bill once a month, start billing twice a month. It's a simple idea with big results.

2. Bill in advance. This works particularly well if you are a service business. Bill for your service fifteen or thirty days in advance.

3. Deliver your product or service more quickly. The faster you can turn around your product or service, the sooner you'll get paid, and the

less money you'll have tied up in "work in progress."

4.   Factor your accounts receivable. If you're really in a cash crunch, you can "sell" your accounts receivable to a factoring company at a discount. You get the cash immediately. This is a short-term solution but an expensive long-term strategy.

5.   Reduce billing errors. Take time on the front end to ensure that your billing is accurate so you do not waste time (and money) on the back end fixing it.

3.   Identify and monitor the key performance indicators related to your cash flow.

For example, you may need to monitor the number of days sales are outstanding, inventory turnover, gross margin, and your current ratio. If these numbers are heading in the wrong direction, take action immediately.

4.   Monitor your budget on a monthly basis.

Each month, take the time to review your budgeted expenses and compare them to what you actually spent. Are you spending above or below budget? Discuss the variances and take action as needed.

5. Review your cash flow statement on a monthly basis.

A cash flow statement identifies how much cash came into the company and how much went out during a specified period. You might be generating a profit, but this statement will show if you're turning that profit into cash fast enough to fund your growth.

It comes down to this: You really need to know your numbers. Unfortunately, most small firms fall short in this area. You might be surprised to know that many midsize firms fall way short here, too. They just don't have the right financial talent on board. Worst case, you can outsource your number crunching to a good bookkeeper or an outsourced CFO firm.

My business coach used to tell me, "Show me a company without numbers, and I'll show you a company that's in trouble." Cash solves problems, he emphasized. Losses create them.

It is the business leader's job to know those numbers, the margins, and what drives them. A competent business leader will look at the critical numbers and the key performance indicators (KPIs) on a daily, weekly, and monthly basis. We will discuss KPIs in chapter 14.

NEED MONEY QUICKLY?

If you find yourself in the unfortunate position of needing money in a pinch and you are shut out of traditional lending sources, you may need to turn to what I call your "love list." Your love list is people who love you the most and have the capacity to lend you the money.

You rank them in order, and you start calling them. You pay them a reasonable interest rate, maybe 10 or 12 percent on their money. They are only lending you the money because (A) they have it and (B) they love you and are willing to lend you the money for six months or a year to help you get out of whatever hole you are in or to give you the bridge capital to enable you to hire salespeople or grow the business.

I had to do this during some dark days at Platinum Capital, the mortgage company I founded after my Student Painter days. We ended up borrowing $1.5 million in total and paid 20 percent interest. Granted, the proposition may have been perceived as risky at the time because we had been suffering some meaningful losses after the liquidity crisis of 1998 and 1999. However, we had confidence in our plan and vision. Although 20 percent was expensive, we were getting over a 100 percent ROE (return on equity), so it made sense to do this to ensure we had enough cash to survive. And we not only survived—we flourished.

I cannot emphasize enough the primacy of cash. I've seen too many businesses go off the rails because they got into a cash crunch. Knowing your numbers and having a solid financial team will keep you "in the money."

Be paranoid about your cash level. Check it daily, if needed. Cash is like oxygen. A short time without it and you are dead.

PEOPLE: BUILD THE BEST TEAM POSSIBLE

If you want to accelerate your growth rate, it is mission critical to have the right people in the right jobs.

I almost always find that firms lack a strong management team. Your current team may have been good enough to get you to where you are today, but deep inside you know you will likely need to upgrade to make the next big jump in growth.

As a quick exercise, take a moment and rate each person on your management team on a scale of one to five, with five being a rock star. Anyone who is not a five should either be managed up to a five in the next ninety days or be respectfully managed out the door.

The fact is, if they are not working out for you, it is likely not working out for them, either. In most cases, exiting your company is the push they need to find a new opportunity that is a much better fit.

When hiring a key person, think about where you want the company to be in twelve to eighteen months. What level of skill do you need to get your company to that point? Then hire that person today.

After more than thirty years experience in building high-growth companies, I have learned the following:

- ➔ Hire the absolute best person for the job, and pay up to get them onboard.

- ➔ Align them with your vision.

- ➔ Agree on what you want the person to get done.

➲ Implement a system of accountability.

➲ Get out of the way, and let them do their job.

For example, at Platinum Capital, I brought on Jack Daly to meaningfully upgrade my team.

Jack Daly

Back then, my partner Brett and I were scrappy entrepreneurs gaining a lot of momentum as we built our business, but we needed to bring in some senior talent to help us scale it. We convinced Jack to join our firm.

Jack had tremendous experience in the mortgage business. He had founded Glenfed Mortgage. He ran the mortgage company at

Glendale Federal Bank, Security Pacific Bank, and Fleet Bank. We knew he was the right guy, and having his level of talent on board was what we needed, but there was one small problem: we could not afford to pay him what he was worth.

We convinced him to join our firm by selling him on the vision of where we were headed. There was no doubt we were going to build our company to over $1 billion. Jack believed in the vision. We gave him a piece of the action, and he became our partner. And yes, we exceeded our $1 billion goal in 2005 and ultimately hit $1.6 billion in 2006.

Beyond offering a piece of the action, here are two other ways to structure the comp package to make it attractive to top achievers when you do not have the budget to offer what they're really worth.

First, develop an attractive "pay for performance" package. In this scenario, you offer a base salary that you can afford and then add a meaningful upside incentive. For example, if you tie your incentive to a result that ultimately generates higher cash flow, you know you'll have the cash to pay the big incentive.

You need to get creative here. Having a meaningful cash incentive is only one piece to the puzzle of attracting top people. Find out what really drives your candidate. Is it all about money? Probably not. How about recognition? How about giving them the ability to run their own profit center within your company? By understanding their motivation and what would get them to jump out of bed in the morning, you can structure the job to meet their needs beyond just putting extra cash in their pocket.

Second, consider a phantom stock type program. Phantom stock is a form of a long-term incentive plan used by businesses to award employees with potential value without stock dilution. It's essentially a type of deferred bonus tied to appreciation in the equity or market value of your company. One of our clients has used this very successfully to increase team compensation and encourage employee retention.

Third, calculate how long it will take you to get a return on your investment. Here is a typical scenario that happens in many businesses. You want to hire more salespeople but can't attract them with a commission only program. Let's say for example, you pay them $5,000 per month draw against commissions, and they typically don't make any sales in the first couple months, but in the third month they generate enough commission to cover their $5,000 draw. Now, you are negative $10,000 from month one and two, plus any hiring expenses and payroll taxes but are even in month three. In months four and five, they generate $10,000 in commissions. You are now at breakeven, and we are off and running.

How many times would you do this? Probably as many as you can if you get similar results. Every business has different margins, sales cycles, some short and some long, and different economics in terms of what kind of draw or salary they need to pay. You can also use the same example and pay them a salary and work backward in terms of what the commission would be. The key here is to hire winners who you believe have a very high probability of achieving the return you are expecting. If they do not achieve your expectations during the three- or six-month probationary period, you just let them go. Do not compromise on hiring top talent, or this formula won't work.

Jack was just one of many top people I hired over the years. I hired my CFO from Indy Bank and then a few years later upgraded to an even stronger guy. The head of credit I hired had spent years working in senior management for Washington Mutual and Countrywide. I also hired several other key players from some of my strongest competitors. By hiring those key people who had been there and done it with much larger firms, I was able to grow my own firm much faster, while maintaining control with systems and processes.

When we begin coaching within a firm, I typically find three areas of major weakness.

1. The leaders may know where they want to go, but they don't really know how to get there, i.e., they don't know how to *make BIG happen!*

2. They don't understand their gross margin and how to positively impact it.

3. They don't have the right people to take them where they need to go.

We, therefore, often begin the relationship by running a planning session with the leadership team. We look for whatever weakness on the team would prevent the company from going where it wants to go. And if that weakness is the leadership team, the company cannot afford to wait until the right person just happens along. It must find the people who have been there, done it, and proved it.

Most businesses simply do not have the talent required to scale. My client, Rich Balot, is one of the largest Verizon dealers in the United States. When I met him, the business was on the verge of bankruptcy. He had just lost $8.5 million, was out of cash, the numbers his CFO was providing him were wrong, and his head of sales, who was a very close friend, simply did not have what it took to turn the business around.

Within short order, we brought in the necessary talent, especially in two key roles—the vice president of sales (one of the best in the country in his industry) and the CFO—and the company went on to grow from a $100 million business on life support to a thriving $330 million in revenue in just three years, with a very meaningful profit of double the industry average.

In early 2015, Rich merged his company with a much larger company, and he is currently the chairman and co-CEO of a $1 billion company.

Another client, Craig Coleman, CEO of ForwardLine, a financial services company, had steady and consistent growth for years. We accelerated that growth by bringing in a strong head of sales, CRO (chief revenue officer), and a CFO. It enabled his company to scale in a big way, and he recently closed on a large private equity deal at a valuation that far exceeded his expectations.

In another example, Ben Hargraves, CEO of Hargraves Urban out of Sydney, Australia, had $9 million in revenue when I met him. In 2015, he grew that to about $15 million. And he is on track to double that in the year ahead. To accomplish this, we brought in a top CFO and a strong chief operating officer from the industry and upgraded several other key roles.

The results are unmistakable. When you have the right people in the right jobs, your revenue will swell. When you bring in top talent, your company will thrive.

KEY RELATIONSHIPS: OWN THEM

Off the top of your head, can you name your five or six most important business relationships? When was the last time you spent quality time with them?

A key relationship is any relationship that would cause a great deal of harm to your company if it went away. As the CEO, you must take responsibility for the key relationships.

Your banker is one of those people with whom you must develop a strong relationship. This is your responsibility as the CEO; this is not just the realm of the financial person on your team. Likewise, as CEO, you need to own your relationships with key vendors and not just leave it to somebody in purchasing.

Several years ago, a client in Canada had the misfortune of failing to get a supply order from a key vendor—and as a result, my client was unable to deliver to his key customer, Costco. This all happened right before Christmas.

Imagine how you would feel if your vendor failed to deliver, putting you in a mess with your most profitable customer. When my client called up that vendor and started screaming at him, he learned that the vendor had sold the product to somebody else at a higher margin. If my client had a deeper relationship with that vendor, I'm confident this would not have happened.

I have learned that the better your relationship becomes with key vendors, the better the pricing and terms you can negotiate. This will drive down the time that your money is outstanding—an essential element of the cash-operating cycle. Once you get really close, they will share with you what your top competitors are doing, new industry trends, and who is on the cutting edge—perhaps letting you test new products before they release to others or maybe even giving you exclusivity for a period of time in a territory or product.

Your key customers are another essential relationship you must groom. Who are the most important customers to the company, the ones who really matter? These are your high-volume and high-margin customers that are growing, and you have a great opportunity to grow your business with them. For our client TaskUs, this is Uber. TaskUs goes out of its way to do everything it can to ensure that Uber is happy and that TaskUs is meeting or exceeding Uber's expectations.

Customers where you have a great opportunity to increase your share of wallet are also candidates for being considered a key relationship. For example, this means those customers that are only doing 10 percent of their business with you, and you have the opportunity to garner a much larger share. Who should develop those relationships? Well, your top salespeople will certainly bring in the business and should manage and develop those accounts. However, it falls upon you as the CEO to make sure those relationships are strong and enduring. After all, salespeople have a way of leaving and taking their business down the street to a competitor.

Other key relationships you must not overlook include the administrators and politicians and their staffs in the municipal and state or federal government. This will be particularly crucial for some industries. Who are the people who might have some say over issues that are important to you? Who are the regulators who could make or break your business? If this is applicable to your business, you, as the CEO, should own these relationships.

It is the responsibility of the CEO to determine which relationships are the most important to the company and how to get closer to those people so those relationships are never lost.

When I was selling mortgage product at Platinum Capital and trying to cut a deal with Bear Stearns, I was told that it bought only from the big guys like Countrywide, Washington Mutual, and Wells Fargo Bank. It did not buy from midsize lenders like me.

Undeterred, I went to find the managing director, and I found him on the trading floor at their headquarters in New York, in the pit with about a thousand loud people. I managed to catch his ear for a few minutes but soon realized that he wasn't going to do business with me.

As I was getting ready to leave, I saw a photograph on his desk showing him crossing the finish line of the New York City Marathon. "Are you a runner?" I asked, and indeed he was—and in a moment we were chatting about our shared passion.

"Next time I come to New York, how about if you and I go for a run in Central Park?" I said, and he agreed. A couple months later, that came to pass. We went out for an hour run and then stopped by Starbucks for coffee and breakfast.

While we were there, we cut a deal—and it was for a pilot program that no one else in the country had been offered. And so we eased into the relationship. We ran a test where they agreed to buy $650 million worth of product from me at seventy-five basis points better than I was getting from anyone else, and they gave me a $70 million credit line at a hundred basis points less than I was paying with my other lenders. The test went well, and that relationship lasted throughout the rest of my time in the mortgage business.

Besides my relationship with Bear Stearns, I had key relationships with GMAC and Citibank. I personally visited them every quarter to enhance the relationship and got to know the people who could positively and negatively impact my business. I made a point to get to know them well all the way up the ladder to the CEO of the operating units.

We also identified a number of real estate firms in our geographic area that we wanted to get closer to so we could build more of a captive audience. We set up joint ventures with them. In doing so, we were able to put our salespeople inside each of their offices. That gave us a heads-up on all the transactions, increasing the probability of getting the deal done. We did that with about twenty-five real estate firms. We also had joint ventures with several builders, enabling us to get a much larger share of the business than we otherwise would have had.

For Rich Balot, who had more than a hundred retail Verizon stores, the key relationship was, of course, with Verizon Wireless. He knew the regional people, but he did not know the senior people at Verizon. I encouraged him to get to know them, all the way up to the C-suite of the entire company.

Due to the key relationships he built, he was able to make some meaningful arrangements with Verizon corporate people that enabled him to scale meaningfully. Whenever a smaller dealer was looking to exit, he was often told about it so he had the opportunity to buy them. From time to time, he was also able to get some incentives that he might not have obtained had he not been as close with the key players. Those relationships had much to do with his firm's quick growth and financial performance.

Rich meticulously nurtured his key relationships by taking an active interest in their lives by texting them on their birthdays and anniversaries, attending sporting events together, and using every opportunity to meet to see each other in person to build quality personal relationships.

Again, the CEO must not abdicate the responsibility for developing those relationships. In addition to nurturing existing key relationships, he or she must also identify new strategic relationships and cultivate those. You cannot just sit by the phone waiting for people to call you. That is not going to happen. Instead, make a list of people you want to get to know, rank them, and start getting to know them. These new relationships could have a massive impact on your success.

NEVER STOP LEARNING: STAY RELEVANT

To compete and survive in the business world, we must never cease to learn. One simple way is to make it a habit to read industry periodicals. Take it a step further and participate in groups like EO, YPO, Vistage, and TEC to continue to sharpen your game and learn from shared experiences with your peers.

The importance of learning and innovative thinking was underscored for me recently when I spent a week with the Young

Presidents Organization attending Singularity University in Silicon Valley. The initiatives there will have a true global impact in the very near future. The vision is to positively impact one billion people in the next decade in one of the world's grand challenges.

Here are a few interesting things I learned from the Singularity University event.

In the 1920s, the average lifespan of a company on the S&P 500 was sixty-seven years. Today, it is fifteen. It is predicted by 2025, 40 percent of Fortune 500 companies will not only no longer be on the list but will be out of business. The very things that made companies successful fifty or sixty years ago are getting in their way today.

It is highly likely that your business will be disrupted. Make sure you are the one creating the disruption. Every week, startups that are threats to traditional business are being launched. They are nimble, and they are fearless. Consider the new-world examples of Airbnb, which is challenging the hotel industry; Uber, which has become a game-changer in transportation in hundreds of cities worldwide; and the meteoric rise of Slack, Snapchat, and other technological brands.

I encourage you to start thinking about innovations in your own businesses. Salim Ismail, author of *Exponential Organizations*, said, "Any company designed for success in the twentieth century is doomed to failure in the twenty-first." Think about that. Is your company's business model outdated? How are you using today's technology to succeed in our fast-changing world?

Find one aspect of your business to develop; you do not want to monkey with the organization as a whole. And you do not need to do it on your own. Talk it over with your advisors or business coach. Familiarize yourself with communities such as Kaggle, which provide a platform for world-class statisticians and data-miners to provide companies with innovative models.

The advances in technology have brought with them opportunities and challenges. We are seeing incredible advancements in medicine, health, and wellness, for example. These disruptive advances in medical science will result in many of us living to age one hundred and beyond. And our kids will live much longer.

Early diagnosis of conditions and diseases will allow doctors to practice preventive medicine rather than reactively treat diseases. The technology is advancing in which 3D printers could be able to reproduce functioning human organs.

And how is this for a game changer: within the next few years, the advancements in brain-reading technology will make it all but impossible to lie without being detected. Another reason for honesty to be the best policy.

When I think about the potential implications of the technological advancements we are seeing today, it seems to me that we are catching up to the science fiction books that captured our imaginations as kids. Most of you have heard of Moore's Law, which (somewhat simplified) states that computer speed and power doubles every two years while costing half as much. A speaker at Singularity put it in perspective. "Within the next ten years, we will have a $1,000 computer with the computational power of the human brain. By 2050, that same $1,000 will buy the computational power of the entire human race."

With such advances in automation and robotics, just what then will all we humans be doing? As it is, 40 percent of the jobs in the US today could be replaced by machine-based algo-rithms. Robots are compelling because they do not care about the minimum wage, they do not use 50 percent more energy when working overtime, and they do not leave early to attend their daughter's soccer game. And if you think worker replacement will be limited to blue-collar jobs, guess again. There is much more to gain by replacing higher-paying, white-collar jobs.

Much of this massive change is happening because of the rise of exponential technology. Authors Peter Diamandis and Steven Kotler in their book, *Bold: How to Go Big, Create Wealth and Impact the World*, developed a framework they call The Six D's of Exponential Technology. It lays out the path exponential technol-ogy takes, and if you are not on the lookout for this technology in your industry, you will regret it:

1. *Digitization.* Anything that can be turned into a one or a zero will be. In other words, if your product or service can be turned into software, it will be.

2. *Deception.* This is a period in which the exponential growth goes mostly unnoticed because it is doubling from a very small base. Here is where if you do not stay on top of your potential competitors—even though they are small—you might wake up one day and discover you are toast.

3. *Disruption.* If you do not respond, you are history. The exponentially growing disruptors will wreak havoc. Just look at what Uber is doing to the taxi business.

4. *Dematerialization.* Eventually, digitization and exponential growth leads to vanishing of the physical goods and services themselves. Consider

that smartphones obliterated the need for a camera, flashlight, GPS, watch, music player, maps, and thousands of other physical goods. Holograms are now dematerializing humans!

5. **Demonetization.** As physical goods go away and everything turns to software, the cost of everything heads toward zero. Look at what Skype did to long-distance phone call costs or what Craigslist did to classified advertising.

6. **Democratization.** Exponential technology levels the playing field. A kid in his garage can create something, load it on the Internet, and, if it becomes popular, it can go viral and become a billion-dollar company virtually overnight. Instagram sold for $1 billion, and they only had thirteen employees. Twenty years ago, you would have needed thousands of employees before you could get a $1 billion valuation.

So how does this voyage into The Matrix affect the businesspeople of today?

Our world is changing faster than ever, and our future is exciting. The next innovation that could disrupt your business may already be in development by the kid described above in his garage. To combat it, you may have to carve off a small staff to work on its own so you can be that "kid in the garage" and be the disruptor, not the disruptee.

In short, we must be endlessly innovative to meet the world's challenges, to remain relevant, and to *make BIG happen!*

Instead of letting yourself be disrupted, why not become the disruptor? Here are nine questions to ask yourself to speed the process of becoming a disruptor:

✥	1. What would it take to be our industry disuptor?
👁	2. What are our competitors doing to disrupt our industry?
📣	3. How do we engage our community or crowd?
🏢	4. How do we scale with virtually no marginal cost?
↗	5. What can we do to leverage assets from the sharing economy?
📊	6. Can we use algorithms to improve our performance?
⇄	7. Who can we partner with to leverage each other's platforms?
👥	8. What can others do to make us the disruptee?
⧖	9. Who owns this effort and how much time is being devoted?

Rapid change is here to stay. Answer these nine questions, and you can stay one step ahead of your competition.

Finally, CEOs need a business coach to challenge them and hold them accountable to building and vetting a plan.

Working with a good coach is like looking in the mirror at who you really are. The coach will point out your blind spots and can help you become a better leader who executes and performs more efficiently. If you do not have a coach today to help you elevate your game, get one—because now, more than ever, those who are not at the top of their game are at risk of sinking to the bottom.

As Eric Hoffer wrote, "In times of change, learners inherit the earth, while the learned find themselves beautifully equipped to deal with a world that no longer exists."

Chapter 4 Action Steps

☑ Focus on the five important things a CEO should spend their time on: vision, cash, people, key relationships, and continuous learning.

☑ Research exponential technology, keep technology startups on your radar, and make sure your firm is staying relevant on the technology side.

☑ Start working on ways your firm can be an industry disruptor instead of being disrupted.

CHAPTER 5

Execute on the Leading Activities

Can you name three activities for your business that meet the following criteria:

1. Completing them at the specified level will help you achieve your HOTs.

2. Completing them is directly within your control.

If you have trouble quickly coming up with those three activities, you are not alone. Most businesses focus on what are called "lag indicators." Lag indicators measure your progress toward achieving a HOT or a goal. They are measures such as number of transactions closed, gross profit, conversion rate, and percentage change in revenue growth or net profit margin.

By contrast, leading activities are the specific actions you can take that will have the greatest effect in directly leading to achieving your HOTs. For example, let's say you are a financial advisor and your HOT is to increase revenue 21 percent for the year. A leading activity might be delivering a retirement planning seminar. This is a leading activity because (A) seminars lead to prospect meetings, and some of those prospects turn into clients who generate new revenue for the firm, and (B) you can control how many retirement planning seminars you deliver. In this example, the lag indicator would be the actual increase in revenue for the year.

The big "a-ha" we often find with CEOs is when they make the switch from focusing on lag indicators to identifying, measuring, and executing on the leading activities. They see the connection between executing on the leading activities and driving the lag indicators.

Archimedes said, "Give me a place to stand, and with a lever I will move the whole world." Leading activities act like a lever. You know that completing the leading activities will give you the greatest leverage toward achieving your HOTs.

The key, however, is to effectively identify the leading activities.

Here are four examples from our coaching clients of HOTs, leading activities, lead measures, and lag measures:

1.   Consulting company

   a. HOT: Increase gross margin to 40 percent.

   b. Leading Activity: Increase the utilization of consultants.

   c. Lead Measure: Increase the utilization of consultants to 85 percent by adjusting the number of full-time employees and using contractors when needed.

d. Lag Measure: Determine actual utilization and gross margin results.

2. SaaS company

a. HOT: Create $50,000 in MRR (monthly reoccurring revenue).

b. Leading Activity: Track number of demos done.

c. Lead Measure: Do 180 demos this quarter.

d. Lag Measure: Close sixty deals this quarter.

3. Transportation company

a. HOT: Reduce repair and maintenance to sixteen cents per mile.

b. Leading Activity: Sell old trucks and replace with fuel-efficient ones.

c. Lead Measure: Sell twelve old trucks and replace them with nine fuel-efficient vehicles.

d. Lag Measure: Determine actual repair and maintenance cost per mile.

4. Wealth management company

a. HOT: Increase new assets under management by $52 million this year.

b. Leading Activity: Deliver twelve retirement planning educational seminars.

    c. Lead Measure: Have 388 people attend the seminars.

    d. Lag Measure: Determine the number of prospect meetings that result from the seminars.

These examples should give you an idea of how you would complete this exercise for your company.

Once you have your leading activities identified, you have to execute them. But here is the rub. Too often, I have seen this thing called "The Knowing–Doing Gap" get in the way. You know what to do, but for some reason, you are just not doing it.

Here are three ways to overcome The Knowing–Doing Gap.

First, go back to the first Make Big Happen question—*What do you want?* If you're not implementing, it is likely what you want is just not compelling enough. So go back and take a hard look at what you want. Modify it. You know you have it right when thinking about it sends a wave of energy through your body. If it makes you yawn, then go back to the drawing board.

Second, get somebody to hold you accountable for following through. If you need a coach, hire one. If you have a friend who can show you some tough love, make arrangements. If you have a dream vacation that you would like to take the family on, tell your spouse you'll only go if you can hit your HOT. I can assure you that your spouse will be pushing you to get the job done.

Third, track your implementation results. If you spend any time around me, you'll hear me say, "If you can't define it, you can't measure it. If you can't measure it, you can't manage it." The mere act of tracking your leading activity leads to momentum. It means you have defined it, you are monitoring it, and, given that you are likely a "high D" on the DISC system, you are competitive and want to get it done.

Now, let me give you three traps to watch out for when you are trying to close The Knowing–Doing Gap:

1. Don't confuse planning with doing.

2. Don't confuse talking with doing.

3. Don't confuse making decisions with doing.

Planning, talking, making decisions—they are all necessary. But ultimately, they are just appetizers. In the end, the only doing is doing.

Kahlil Gibran, a Lebanese novelist, poet, and artist said, "A little knowledge that acts is worth infinitely more than much knowledge that is idle." Take that to heart.

Chapter 5 Action Steps

- ☑ Identify the leading activities that will lead to achieving your HOTs.

- ☑ Identify the lead measure and lag measure to track how well you're executing on the leading activities.

- ☑ Be aware of and close The Knowing–Doing Gap.

CHAPTER 6

Ask Better Questions

Remember the Polaroid camera? It resulted from a three-year-old girl asking, "Why do we have to wait for the picture?" Ask better questions and you'll get better answers—and it will help you determine what you need to do.

THREE PROVOCATIVE QUESTIONS

Imagine you are starting a new company to compete with the one you operate now. With that scenario, you can reinvent your business model by asking three provocative questions:

1. What am I doing now that I would stop doing in my new company?

2. What am I not doing now that I would start doing in my new company?

3. How would I compete to try to put my old company out of business?

MAKE BIG HAPPEN | 83

In January 2010 when I began working with the people at Grasshopper, a virtual phone system provider for entrepreneurs, we went through this exercise. We created a fictitious company and answered those questions on a whiteboard. The consensus was: "That's pretty cool. We want that company instead of the one we have."

And so the question became how to move from A to B. We started redesigning and making tweaks to the model we had built. Then we started to build the organizational structure. We found some holes in it that we needed to fill. It was a painful moment when one of the guys in the room realized his name did not show up on the new organizational structure, but we recognized that we needed somebody else to fill that role.

Over the next year, we replaced every person on the management team except for one—the new COO, Don Schiavone, who was a rock star. We brought in some strong players in marketing, technology, and finance, and that enabled the company to grow dramatically. The firm grew twenty-one quarters in a row and beat the plan for nineteen consecutive quarters.

The plan worked. Grasshopper was sold to Citrix in May 2015 for over $170 million, enabling the founders to have a meaningful liquidity event.

Regardless of where your business is in its lifecycle, periodically ask yourself these three provocative questions. It will ensure you stay one step ahead of any competitor or new technology that could put you out of business.

THE FIVE WHYS

The Three Provocative Questions are an excellent frame to rethink your business. They are used on a strategic level to orient your business toward its best opportunities.

By contrast, the Five Whys are more tactical. They force you to get to the root of a problem so you can fix it once and for all.

The idea is simple. If you have a problem, ask the question "why?" five times to understand what has happened. The technique was developed by Taiichi Ohno, the father of the Toyota Production System, as a problem-solving tool.

The Five Whys Technique from Taiichi Ohno

When confronted with a problem, have you ever stopped and asked why five times? It is difficult to do even though it sounds easy. For example, suppose a machine stopped functioning:

1. Why did the machine stop? (There was an overload, and the fuse blew.)

2. Why was there an overload? (The bearing was not sufficiently lubricated.)

3. Why was it not lubricated sufficiently? (The lubrication pump was not pumping sufficiently.)

4. Why was it not pumping sufficiently? (The shaft of the pump was worn and rattling.)

5. Why was the shaft worn out? (There was no strainer attached, and metal scrap got in.)

Repeating "why" five times, like this, can help uncover the root problem and correct it. If this procedure were not carried through, one might simply replace the fuse or the pump shaft. In that case, the problem would recur within a few months. The Toyota Production System has been built on the practice and evolution of this scientific approach. By asking and answering "why" five times, we can get to the real cause of the problem, which is often hidden behind more obvious symptoms.

Imagine how you could apply the Five Whys in your business. Let's say you missed your monthly sales number by 5 percent. The conversation between you and your sales manager might go like this.

1. Why did we fall 5 percent short?
   (We made fewer sales calls this month.)

2. Why did we make fewer sales calls this month?
   (We had fewer leads to work this month.)

3. Why did we have fewer leads to work this month?
   (We sent fewer email offers.)

4. Why did we send fewer email offers?
   (We were short staffed.)

5. Why were we short staffed?
   (We didn't plan well for two people who were on vacation.)

If you stopped asking "why?" after the first question, you might have thought the solution to the problem was to make more sales calls next month. But in reality, you had to ask five "whys" to realize the fewer calls was driven by lack of planning for two people who were on vacation. If you do not fix the vacation planning process, then the call shortfall problem will reappear in the future.

Now, I can hear you saying, "This would sound childish if I asked 'Why?' five times to my senior people." Let me just say this. Try it. You will get to the root of problems faster and fix them for good.

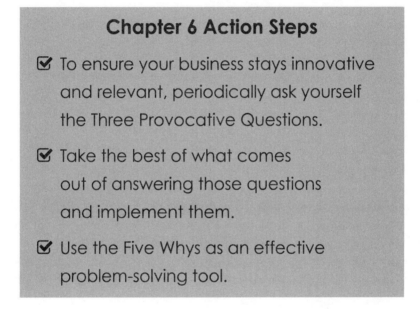

Chapter 6 Action Steps

- ☑ To ensure your business stays innovative and relevant, periodically ask yourself the Three Provocative Questions.

- ☑ Take the best of what comes out of answering those questions and implement them.

- ☑ Use the Five Whys as an effective problem-solving tool.

CHAPTER 7

Enhance Your Thinking

Over the last several years, we have had the opportunity to coach some of the top entrepreneurial CEOs in the world. These are leaders who, on average, have been able to grow their companies' profitability by 185 percent over two years and by more than 550 percent over three years. And over four years, our clients have averaged a revenue Compounded Annual Growth Rate (CAGR) of 40 percent, year after year.

How does that happen? Not only do they follow CEO Coaching International's best practices methodology with relentless focus and discipline, but we also choose clients who we believe have what it takes to deliver and execute on what we talk about. They have the ambition, the drive, and the confidence. In working with these superstars, we have learned how they think, how they act, and what they expect.

Through my years of coaching top CEOs, I have discovered that there are specific traits that successful CEOs all have in common. These are the pillars that all CEOs should think about if they expect to rise to the top.

THINK BIG

These guys think big without limits. One client of mine was twenty-seven years old when I started coaching him, and he has a forty-year plan to be a billionaire. That is thinking big.

One of the simplest ways to think big is to complete the "Add a Zero" exercise. All you do is take one of your key metrics, add a zero to it, and then discuss what you have to do to *make BIG happen!*

For example, if your annual revenue is $20 million, add a zero and you get $200 million. If your current largest client is $50,000 per year, add a zero and you get $500,000. You get the idea.

The magic happens when you discuss what you have to do to go from $20 million in revenue to $200 million or from $50,000 clients to $500,000 clients. You have to completely change your approach to achieving the "times ten" jump because incremental thinking will not get you there. You must go exponential.

By pursuing the "times ten" leap, you will dump your current "let's grow 15 percent per year" strategies and force yourself to develop new "exponential" strategies that will take you to warp speed. Most likely, this will involve turning part of your business into software that can be infinitely scaled.

ALWAYS SHOW CONFIDENCE

Top performers have confidence. They have the ability to make those tough decisions. They believe in themselves and in their ability to execute on their vision.

Suiting up to play tuba at an annual State of the Company meeting.

During some very dark days at Platinum Capital, I hired the Fountain Valley High School band to play at one of our annual State of the Company meetings. I was the first one out on the stage, and although I am a relatively short guy, I was holding the biggest tuba. Then, as the leader of my company's band (and dressed in the high school band uniform), I delivered my state of the company address.

I believe that nothing great was ever achieved without adversity and the desire to march on, and I wanted my employees to believe the same. So when I came marching out with the band, my point was that we were going to continue to build a great company, no matter how ugly things seemed.

Despite the fact that I could not meet payroll, my job was to inspire people to do their best. If I had come out on stage looking devastated from the tough times and feeling sorry for myself, my staff might have wondered, "Are we going to make it?" No matter how hard it gets, it's your job as the leader to continue to look at the glass as half full, not half empty.

TAKE CALCULATED RISKS

As the CEO, you must decide when it's time to take a risk and when it's time to be more conservative. Better yet, do what my former YPO forum buddy Mohnish Pabrai does. He told me the kind of bet he likes to take is one where: "Heads I win, tails I don't lose much."

He is the author of two books, *The Dhandho Investor: The Low-Risk Value Method to High Returns* and *Mosaic: Perspectives on Investing.* He once bought a lunch on eBay with Warren Buffett. It cost him $650,000. But Warren Buffett had been his idol for many years. He wanted to be like Warren Buffett, and he wanted to be close to Warren Buffett. He figured that buying the lunch would give him that opportunity to hobnob with him and his friend and partner, Charlie Munger. It was a calculated bet. It would be a chance to learn, build a relationship with them, and get some publicity. It would enable him to sell out his fund.

Reed Hastings, the CEO of Netflix, made a calculated bet when he brought streaming into the business. That was a big winner. He also made a calculated bet when he started monkeying with pricing. That was not as popular, and he got himself in the doghouse with his customers. Hastings continues to advance the ball for Netflix, and he has done an amazing job.

BE COURAGEOUS

As the leader, your team looks to you to have the courage to make the hard decisions. At times, you are going to be unpopular when making those decisions, but you must do what you believe is right.

These tough decisions might involve a major change in company direction, such as eliminating a long-time management member whose skills the company has outgrown, or shutting down a facility or product line.

My colleague and good friend Michael Maas built a company up to $175 million in revenue before some bad business decisions threw it into a near-death situation. He told me about how he and his leadership team had to find the courage to be fully transparent with their stakeholders about their dire situation. It was humbling to tell the stakeholders how deep the troubles were, but by having the courage to be honest and transparent, his team won their support. Within a few years, the company's revenue had grown to nearly $300 million, and the company was sold for a nine-figure number.

MAINTAIN THE RIGHT ATTITUDE

CEOs are smart, but they are often not the smartest person at the company. However, one trait they almost always have is the right attitude. They realize having the right mental attitude is more important than having the right mental capabilities.

Now do not get me wrong. CEOs do not walk around the office spouting off positive mental attitude platitudes. Instead, they do this:

- ➲ They carefully choose the words they use to send the right message.

- ➲ They prefer optimism over pessimism.

- ➲ They hang around positive people and avoid

energy-drainers.

- ⊙ They are grateful for what they have instead of envying their neighbor.

- ⊙ They think before acting out of fear or frustration.

And perhaps most importantly, CEOs should have an attitude similar to what Admiral James Stockdale described to Jim Collins in Collins' book *Good to Great*. When asked how he survived more than seven brutal years as a POW during the Vietnam War, Stockdale replied, "You must never confuse faith that you will prevail in the end—which you can never afford to lose—with the discipline to confront the most brutal facts of your current reality, whatever they might be."

I'm not suggesting that CEOs confront the same hardship as Stockdale endured. Far from it. Rather, I am suggesting that whatever situation you face, whether it is having to fire staff, close a facility, or stare down bankruptcy, adopting the attitude Stockdale described is key.

CEOs must combine an unshakable faith that things will workout in the end with a laser focus on the reality of the current situation. When faced with difficult times, balancing long-term faith with short-term urgency is a good combination.

FOCUS ON YOUR HOME LIFE

Building and running a successful company is extremely hard. Yet many leaders take comfort in knowing that their home life is stable, and they enjoy time with their family as a welcomed respite from the rigors of work. Of course, you cannot take a healthy home life for granted. Those who make family a priority—even during the most intense periods of running the business—reap immeasurable rewards.

On the other hand, leaders who turn their personal life into a mess almost always pay the price for it in their business life.

A great (but sad) example here is Tiger Woods.

In 2009, he won six times on the PGA Tour. He led the PGA Tour in prize winnings for the ninth time. His peers voted him player of the year for the tenth time in his fourteen years as a pro. Since turning pro, he had won fourteen major championships and was threatening to break Jack Nicklaus' record of eighteen major championships.

Then the wheels fell off.

In late November 2009, Woods was exposed as a serial cheater. His wife chased him out of their multimillion-dollar home while wielding a golf club, and Woods smashed his Cadillac trying to escape.

He has never been the same golfer since.

Six years after that nightmarish turn of events, Woods was a shadow of his former self. His world ranking had fallen from #1 to below #400. He won zero major championships. And in the fall of 2015, he went in for his second back surgery in eighteen months, and the prognosis for him returning to his winning ways was bleak.

Clearly, the mess in his personal life affected his golf game—and took a huge toll on his body. Poor thinking on his part has had a devastating effect on his career ... and on his legacy.

Woods is not the first nor will he be the last high achiever whose personal problems lead to work problems.

One of our clients went through a divorce and a lawsuit that cost him a fortune. During that time, his business was days from running out of cash.

Not all family issues that affect the business relate to personal failings. A client and good friend lost his wife to lung cancer. He stepped out of his business for about two years to take care of her. It hurt the business, but of course, it was the right thing to do.

And let's not forget sick kids, sibling rivalries, family struggles in family businesses, parent health issues, and sickness or death of key employees—all of which affect our work life.

My point is this: family first. Long after your business is gone, your family will remain. It is the one constant that will be there through the ups and downs of business. Your family will outlive your work career. Take care of them.

Chapter 7 Action Steps

☑ Make a conscious effort to improve your thinking by thinking big, showing confidence, taking calculated risks, displaying courage, and maintaining the right attitude.

☑ Do no get so caught up in your work that you ignore your family. Take care of them.

CHAPTER 8

Create an
Energizing Culture

A leader with vision pays close attention to the quality of their company culture, and they view their company culture as an investment, not an expense.

The CEO is the chief energizing officer. He or she is the one who sets the frame for the company's culture, who develops the big vision, and who gets everyone to buy into it.

Focusing on company culture generates a huge return on investment.

A ten-year study by Harvard professor John Kotter compared public companies with a strong focus on corporate culture to companies without a strong focus. The conclusion?

 Firms that had a strong focus on corporate culture increased their revenue by 682 percent, compared to just 166 percent for non-culture focused firms.

 Their stock price increased by 901 percent, versus 74 percent.

- They saw a huge gain in net income: 756 percent, versus 1 percent.

- Their job growth increased 282 percent, versus 36 percent.

A "cool" company culture ultimately will attract the right kind of employees—but it's important to make sure that those who come through the door are a good match for the culture of the organization you are trying to build.

Netflix is a great example of how to use culture as a competitive advantage.

The Netflix culture slide deck made an appearance on the Internet in 2009 and immediately created a sensation. Facebook COO Sheryl Sandberg said, "It may well be the most important document ever to come out of the Valley."

So what is in it?

According to an article found at FirstRound.com, "It's a living set of 'behaviors and skills' that the Netflix management team updated continuously and fastidiously. And it drives toward a single point: a company is like a pro sports team, where good managers are good coaches, and the goal is to field stars in every position."

To give you a flavor, here is an excerpt on hard work from the Netflix culture slide deck.

HARD WORK—NOT RELEVANT

- We do not measure people by how many hours they work or how much they are in the office.

- We do care about accomplishing great work.

- Sustained B-level performance, despite "A for effort," generates a generous severance package, with respect.

- Sustained A-level performance, despite minimal effort, is rewarded with more responsibility and great pay.

How does this compare to your company?

Visit www.slideshare.net/reed2001/culture-1798664 to read the "Netflix culture deck" in its entirety. It will spark some great ideas for you.

The phenomenal success of Netflix in recent years is due in large part to the culture they created, fostered, and communicated. Ironically, the chief architect of the Netflix culture, Patty McCord, ended up losing her job when she was no longer a fit for the culture she helped create.

HIRE "CULTURAL FIT" PEOPLE

Making bad hires is costly. According to the Society for Human Resource Management, turnover can cost a company between 50 percent to 60 percent of the person's salary. Take time on the front end to hire well so you don't pay for it on the back end.

Start by hiring people who are a cultural fit for your company. Now, this may seem obvious, but before you can hire people who fit your culture, you must be able to define and articulate what your culture is. And anyone who is in a position to hire should be clear on this, too.

What is your culture? What are the core beliefs, attitudes, and behaviors expected and embedded in your company? In fact, this would be a good exercise at your next leadership team meeting. Take five minutes and ask each person to write down how they would describe the company's culture. Then read each one. You may be shocked at the result.

Once there is clarity here, start weaving this understanding into your hiring process. For example, if your culture is highly entrepreneurial, look for candidates who have exhibited strong initiative or who have succeeded in other companies known for their entrepreneurial atmosphere.

You can improve your odds of hiring people who are a cultural fit by asking the right questions and using assessments.

Here are a few questions you might ask.

- ❯ What type of culture do you think is the best fit for you?
- ❯ What does your ideal workplace look like?
- ❯ What business values are important to you?
- ❯ What do you find attractive about our company?
- ❯ What's your impression of our culture, and what do you like/dislike about it?
- ❯ What is it about you that you think you could bring to our company that would mesh well with our culture?
- ❯ Tell me about a prior work experience where you were not a strong cultural fit. Why was it a bad fit?

Regarding assessments, I like the ones that separately measure how you perform under normal circumstances and how you perform under pressure. They also measure what drives or motivates you.

You can learn more about the behavior and motivator assessment we use at www.ceocoachinginternational.com/tools.

One of the best ways to find new employees who are likely to fit your culture is to get referrals from your existing employees. Your employees know what the company is like, and they are in a good position to refer friends who are well suited for what you have built.

To speed up the referral process, offer referral bonuses to employees. At Platinum Capital, we paid $10,000 to employees who recommended a salesperson that we ended up hiring.

We would not pay that $10,000 straight up front, though. We gave half of it to the employee who referred the new hire when the new hire had closed his or her tenth transaction. Since we made $1,500 per transaction, we had already made $15,000.

We gave the second half of the $10,000 when the new hire had closed the twentieth transaction. By the time we paid the total referral fee, we already made $30,000. We could have gone to a search firm and paid 25 percent of the first year's income, but this was cheaper, it motivated our employees, and it reinforced our pay for performance culture.

We paid a lot of attention to motivating employees at Platinum Capital—and that helped shape the culture, too.

For example, many firms throw a going-away party for people when they leave, even when they are going to work for a competitor. When Jack Daly joined our firm, he recommended we start throwing parties for the new hires. And that is what we did.

On the first day a new employee joined us, they were greeted with streamers and balloons. Their business cards were sitting

Celebrate all new hires with parties.

on their desk along with a coffee cup with the company logo on it. They would get a welcome note from the CEO, and we would have a luncheon for them in celebration of their joining our company.

We would also have an orientation and integration plan that included lunch with me, the CEO. Once a month, I would have lunch with ten people. Each person would share a little bit about his or her background. And then I would share a little bit about my background and the company's history, our values, and our vision.

I got to know them. They got to know me. And they got to know each other. New employees could make friends throughout the organization very quickly. Studies by the Gallup Organization have shown having a friend at work generates numerous benefits to the employee and the company, so fostering friendships is definitely worth the effort.

RECOGNIZE EMPLOYEES

Recognizing employees is also a key part in shaping company culture.

We all know employees thrive when they get recognition. At Platinum Capital, we used to give away a convertible 500SL Mercedes to the top salesperson each month.

Imagine coming in to work and having the opportunity to drive away with a 500SL. The catch was they only got to keep the car for one month. It was my old car, and it was on lease. The lease cost me $1,000 a month, and the insurance was $300. My total cost was $1,300 a month.

The first time we launched this contest, we got about fifty additional loans. With a $1,500 profit per loan, the additional $75,000 in net income was an excellent return on a $1,300 investment.

The salespeople fought hard for the chance to drive that convertible Mercedes for the month. It was so successful that we introduced a convertible Mustang into the program and let people compete on trying to win that, too. It was a good contest for employees whose average age was twenty-four.

I regularly sent out personal note cards to employees. Yes, it takes time and effort. But every single person in the company—all five hundred or so—would get a personal birthday card from me, handwritten and signed. Everyone would get an anniversary card from me on the hiring date, too.

The "thinking big" elephant.

We had a large ceramic elephant in our lobby that stood for "thinking big," and whenever somebody won an award, he or she would get a photo taken with me as one of us sat on the elephant. I would upload the photo to Shutterfly.com and send it to the award winner.

Our people usually kept those cards. I would notice, as I walked through the office, that most of the desks had pictures of me with the new employee. I also tried to write an additional five notecards per month just thanking people for making an extra effort or recognizing an accomplishment.

We emphasized the importance of catching people doing something right. Anyone could go up to the receptionist, ask for a note card and balloon, and give it to the person meriting such appreciation.

Many companies offer President's Club awards. My client, Sheldon Wolitski of The Select Group, recently returned from taking his winning team to Turks and Caicos for an amazing celebration after setting another record year, having grown more than eightfold in four years.

Of course, your celebrations do not have to involve expensive travel. You could do a cookout in the parking lot or a dunk tank featuring … you! Be creative.

The bottom line here is, go out of the way to recognize your employees. It pays cultural dividends.

GENERATE FREE PUBLICITY

In this age of social media, it's easier than ever to get publicity for your company. And in a competitive hiring environment, having some positive press puts your company higher up the list of desirable places to work.

In earlier days, we invited local politicians to celebrate our company anniversaries and to support us when we did company charitable work. We even invited them to our company picnic.

the BUSINESS CONNECTION

An Award Winning Publication of the Irvine Chamber of Commerce   Volume 14, No. 10 ■ October 1998

Business Spotlight **Platinum celebrates 5 year anniversary with 10,000% growth**

Platinum Capital Group, a specialty retail mortgage company, opened in 1993 just six months before the collapse of California's real estate market. "Outside the box" thinking helped Platinum survive the recession, and they were on their way to major expansion when their general manager abruptly quit and took with him many key personnel to open a competing business. Left with only a skeleton crew, CEO Mark Moses' first memo to his employees read, "Nothing great was ever achieved without adversity. Let's march on together toward greatness."

Platinum began hiring feverishly in order to meet the demand for their newly introduced 125 loan product and began to grow when adversity struck again.

After a move to a larger facility, an explosion destroyed the company's telephone and computer systems and made it necessary for employees to evacuate the building. Electric company and fire department officials determined the damage could not be repaired for at least three weeks. Knowing that a delay of this magnitude

the computers and telephones. Seventeen hours after the fire, Platinum's employees returned to work and were met with coffee, juice, muffins, and t-shirts which read "Platinum is on fire." Most importantly, they had telephones and computers that worked, and they were back in business.

Today, Platinum has four offices in Irvine, Manhattan Beach, La Mirada and Encino and employs more than 300 people. It is licensed in 45 states and is one of the fastest growing retail mortgage companies in the county. In fact, they've seen a 10,000% growth rate in just five years. Platinum was named 1998 Entrepreneur of the Year by Ernst and Young, was a finalist in the Small Business Administration's Small Business Person of the Year, and was recently awarded the Blue Chip Initiative Award by Mass Mutual and the U.S. Chamber of Commerce. This award recognizes companies with 5-400 employees that have overcome adversities, seized opportunities and succeeded. "These first five years have been fun,"

Platinum Capital Group's Irvine management team fired up the grills to serve their employees lunch to celebrate the company's five year anniversary. From left to right are Al Tello, representing Senator Ross Johnson's office; Rob Hill, chief financial officer; Mark Moses, CEO (Chief Energizing Officer); Jack

I even rode an elephant and made the local news for my bold action (more on this later). We let the media know about all such events, and we let them know whenever we were up for an award.

Think about your business. What are ways you could generate free publicity? This would be a good topic for a monthly planning meeting.

SET HUGE OUTRAGEOUS TARGETS (HOTS)

At Platinum Capital, we set HOTs, and when we met them, we celebrated big.

Over the years, we celebrated in many different cities and locales. If we had a contest where we were going to San Francisco, we would dress up the office to look like San Francisco. If we had a contest where we were going on a three-day cruise down to Ensenada, Mexico, we would dress up the office so it looked like a cruise ship.

Once we held a contest in which we agreed to take all of the employees—at the time, about three hundred people—to Las Vegas for the weekend, all expenses paid, if we were able to meet a Huge Outrageous Target. By the last day of the quarter, the team achieved 25 percent higher results than in any quarter in the company's history.

WE HAD A KILLER PARTY IN VEGAS

People wondered, "Wow, what did that cost to take all those people to Vegas?" The question they should have asked was: "What did the company earn as a result of hitting the Huge Outrageous Target, and what was the impact on the culture?" We made multiples of what we spent—and we had set a new high-water mark that we could strive to beat in future quarters. We showed our people what was possible.

HOTs force you to set a very important goal, so that once it is achieved, there would be a breakthrough for your company. And it is these breakthroughs that become part of company lore.

Mark's company took all 300 of its employees to Las Vegas for exceeding its Huge Outrageous Target.

GIVE POWER TO THE PEOPLE

A big part of motivation, besides reward and recognition, is empowerment. Employees should be empowered to do what is in the best interest of the customer. They should be able to use their best judgment without having to go through several levels of management for approval. They should be able to make decisions on the spot and ask for forgiveness later.

For example, Nordstrom's has just one rule in their employee handbook. It says employees are to provide outstanding customer service at all times—and in doing so, they are to use their own best judgment in all situations. Pretty simple.

Ritz-Carlton is another example of a company that takes customer service to heart. Most employees know money has been specifically budgeted for use in solving customer problems. You could be a valet attendant, a waiter or waitress, a maid, or a front-desk clerk. It does not matter. If a customer is unhappy, the staff has a budget to help solve that customer's pain right there on the spot. The St. Regis in Punta Mita, Mexico, is the best I have ever seen at this.

In too many companies, satisfying the customer involves ribbons of red tape. How about your company?

What kind of culture are you creating? Are you enabling your people to think for themselves and empowering them to do what is in the best interest of both the firm and the customer? Or are you micromanaging them and not allowing them to think independently? Do you trust your people?

Grasshopper gives employees unlimited time off—and they do not abuse it. Each employee is allowed to spend 20 percent of the time working on his or her own projects to help innovate and advance the firm. They get flex-time to work from home.

That kind of culture makes people happy.

It has enabled Grasshopper to grow dramatically year after year. The people there are excited about coming to work. You can feel it in the air from the moment you walk in. And the excitement, as for all companies with a great culture, translates to performance.

When you show confidence like these companies do in their employees, few people will abuse it. And in the end, everybody wins—employees, customers, and the company.

MAKE IT FUN

It's also important to make the work environment fun. At Platinum Capital, we had five core values:

1. Do the right thing.
2. Provide awesome service.
3. Develop lasting relationships.
4. Show mutual respect.
5. Have fun.

Frankly, if I could not have fun, I did not want to be there, so I made every effort to build a cool culture and provide a fun atmosphere for work.

I often run into former employees who tell me that their time with us at Platinum Capital was the most fun they ever had in their working life. "If you're ever hiring again," they say, "please hire me."

Zappos is similar. They have ten core values, one of which is, "Create fun and a little weirdness."

Let's not forget Southwest Airlines. One of their core values is "Fun-LUVing Attitude." And if you have ever flown on Southwest, you know they are not kidding.

Or how about Señor Frog's restaurants?

When you walk in, they put a medallion around your neck. The medallion says that if their food and service do not meet your standards, please lower your standards.

On their website, they say,

If we were to take out a personal ad, we'd describe ourselves as fun, outgoing, energetic, and good looking. The good-looking part might be a stretch, but the other words fit us perfectly. If you've ever been to a Señor Frog's, you already know that we're a place where people of all backgrounds hang together, dance, sing, and basically act the way they want—without worrying about silly rules and regulations. Our philosophy is simple: have fun. Let yourself go. Throw caution to the wind. Do something daring. When you're at Señor Frog's, you're gonna smile—even if we have to hold you down and tickle you (which we've been known to do).

The restaurant franchise goes out of its way to let customers and employees know, when you are *at Señor Frog's*, you are going to have some fun. It has become their culture, and this culture brings back the customers and boosts performance.

With employees spending half their waking hours at work, you have to throw some fun in there. Find ways to bring some fun into your workplace.

With the business clarity in place, let's turn to igniting your enthusiasm for living the life of your dreams.

Chapter 8 Action Steps

☑ Get clear on what your culture is, and be able to effectively communicate it.

☑ Focus on hiring people who fit your culture.

☑ Proactively work on reinforcing your culture and rewarding behavior that exemplifies it

☑ Have Fun!

CHAPTER 9

Give Back

The famous investor John Templeton was often asked what the greatest investment he ever made was. His answer was simple, "tithing."

Templeton said, "In all my years of investment counseling, there was only one investment which never proved faulty, and that was tithing—giving at least 10 percent of your income to churches and charities. In all my history, I have never seen a family who tithed for as long as ten years that didn't become both prosperous and happy. That is the best investment anyone can select."

Likewise, I've worked with many successful entrepreneurs and CEOs who are generous givers. And I'm not just talking money.

Giving your time and energy to causes and organizations you strongly believe in not only benefits those you are helping, but it also benefits you. As humans, we are wired to give. Giving makes us feel good.

Over the years, I've been very active in giving back to several organizations that are important to me. Here are a few examples:

- I spent ten years on YPO's Orange County Chapter board, including being chairman, three years on the Pacific Regional Board, and six years on committees of the International Board.

- I founded and chaired twelve YPO father-daughter and father-son events and chaired various other events for YPOers around the world.

- I chaired YPO's M2Mx (Member to Member Exchange), which enables members of YPO, WPO, and EO to connect with each other on any topic that they need help with. I also had a book written about the M2Mx that was distributed to all members worldwide.

- I spent years on EO Orange County's board and came back in as president to lead the charge to successfully turn the chapter around when it was struggling.

- I spent several years on the board of the Southern California Entrepreneurship Academy that helped young entrepreneurs.

- For years, at both Platinum Capital and at Student Painters, we regularly supported Olive Crest Home for Abused Children.

- I spent six years on the board of the Children's Hospital of Orange County and helped raise hundreds of thousands of dollars for the hospital and got many of my high-profile friends involved.

My family has been active, too. Our son Mason, with help from his sister Darien, raised $3,723 for the Children's Hospital of Orange County through a lemonade stand. Mason then raised another $3,400 online. My wife, Ivette, spent several years on the Orangewood Foundation helping abused and neglected kids.

Mark's son, Mason (left), and daughter, Darien (right), present a check to the Children's Hospital of Orange County.

WHY GIVE BACK?

Besides helping other people, giving back has numerous benefits.

It connects you to new people. When you get involved in an organization, whether it is business, social, or religious, you come in contact with people you might not normally meet. I have made some great connections over the years from my volunteer work, and my personal and professional life has greatly benefitted from them.

It gives you a new perspective. When you are volunteering and helping the less fortunate in society, it really puts life in perspective. I'm sure many people reading this are reasonably financially stable and not worried about putting food on the table or having a comfortable place to sleep tonight. But when you come in contact with people for whom those worries are real, it really makes you feel grateful for your life. And it makes you feel grateful that you can use your time, talents, and resources to help those who are less fortunate.

It's good for your mind and body. Business can be tough, and it's so easy to get caught up in your own little world. Yet, giving back and helping others can give you a sense of accomplishment and purpose that may be lacking elsewhere in your life.

Giving makes you happy. A study from the London School of Economics found that the more people volunteer, the happier they were. I'm sure you can relate to this. Think about the last time you volunteered for a special cause. You probably felt a lot better during and after the event than you did going into it.

A cynical person might say leaders give back because it's a way to gain influence and power. And for some, that might be the case. My advice is simple. Give your time and resources to those organizations that really resonate with you, the ones that you feel good about or have some connection to.

Do not use giving back or volunteering as a cover for trying to extract favors or generate new business. Instead, give out of gratefulness. Give out of an innate desire to help people who are less fortunate. As I once heard a religious leader say, "Give until it feels good."

I've found that the more I give of my time and resources, the more good things tend to happen. This concept even permeates how we coach. Before we take on a new client, our coaches spend a substantial amount of time learning about the potential client and offering coaching advice during the "get to know each other" phase.

And while not everyone we talk to turns into a client, we all benefit from the conversation, even though no money changes hands.

Like dropping a rock in a pond, there's a ripple effect to giving. You may only see the benefit to the person or people you are directly helping, but undoubtedly many more receive some benefit, too.

If giving back is not part of your life right now, find a way to start small. You may find the idea of giving back becomes contagious.

Chapter 9 Action Steps

☑ Begin to appreciate the idea that the best investment you can make is to be more giving.

☑ If you have been modest in giving back, consider a way you can start small with an organization or cause that is important to you and increase your giving.

NEXT QUESTION

So far, we have discussed how to figure out what you want and identified key things you should do to get what you want. Next, we'll delve into what could get in the way of achieving what you want and *making BIG happen!*

QUESTION 3

what could **get** in the **way**?

Watch Your Blind Spots

We all have blind spots—damaging behaviors that everyone but ourselves can see clear as day. For CEOs, these blind spots create unwelcome consequences: they corrupt decision making, reduce our scope of awareness, and sabotage business results.

CEOs deal with massive change and cope with stressful situations every day. Added to this is the belief that strong leaders should have all the answers, should know what to do, and should be able to handle these challenges alone. However, only the most confident leaders are willing to surround themselves with people who will point out what they're doing wrong—and reward them for their honesty.

After years of working with CEOs, you start to recognize a few recurring themes. Here are twelve CEO blind spots I encounter and some coaching to help you course correct if any are your blind spots:

1. ## Not effectively communicating your vision—or worse, not having one

You may be clear on where you want the company to go—or not. Unfortunately, many CEOs are blind to the fact that few employees have any clarity. Twitter is a great example. The product is everywhere, yet nine years into its existence, the company's leaders were still struggling to come up with a vision for the firm. Was it a leading breaking news source? A B2B or B2C marketing service? An easy way to follow the latest antics of the Kardashians? While the leaders may have thought they had a clear vision, Twitter users and Wall Street investors were rather clueless.

What to do:

Develop a vision. Make it accessible throughout the organization through both internal and external communication. Share it at your regularly scheduled company meetings. Reinforce it at every opportunity. If you err, err on the side of over communicating.

2. ## Not effectively communicating your company's value proposition—or worse, not having one

An overwhelming majority—85 percent—of CEOs say their employees can't clearly state the company's value proposition. Unfortunately, only 20 percent of leadership teams can communicate a common value proposition, according to an article from *Inc.* magazine. If your employees cannot communicate your value proposition, then you cannot expect your customers to understand it, either.

Too often, I find that companies think they have a value proposition, but when I question them about it, it is like a marshmallow—all fluff. Pretend you're a customer and have one of your team members share your company's value proposition with you. Are you buying it?

Value propositions are not just sentences strung together that make a great story. Some of the best stories are fairy tales, and your value proposition could be one of them. If your value proposition cannot stand up to serious scrutiny, fix it.

What to do:

Structure your business so that you have a legitimate value proposition that customers can understand and place value on. Then, similar to the vision above, communicate it regularly throughout the organization.

3. Not paying close enough attention to cash

As I mentioned in chapter 4, you must pay extremely close attention to your cash situation. Even though you may be growing like a weed, you could "grow broke" if you do not monitor your cash flow. Cash flow management is not just for the finance department. CEOs must roll up their sleeves and maintain a deep understanding of how the firm turns a dollar of business investment into cash in the bank—and how quickly it does that.

What to do:

Work with your finance person and make sure you fully understand the cash-operating cycle of your company and how to optimize it. Review your cash position as frequently as daily, depending on your business situation.

4. Not delegating enough

As the organization grows, the role of the CEO changes. The CEO's role tends to start off focused on the product or service and then turns to customer development and later to company development. Over time, the CEO role has only a few activities that really matter:

- Setting the company vision and culture
- Monitoring the company cash level
- Hiring the right people in the right jobs
- Cultivating key relationships
- Staying current through continuous learning

Everything else should be delegated to the team. Harvey Mackay said it well, "When you grow, you have to know when to let go. You have to know when to delegate down so you can rise up."

Holding on to things you should no longer personally manage is one of the surest ways to put a chokehold on the growth of your company.

What to do:

Write down a bullet-point list of everything you do. Then go through the list and objectively answer these questions for each item:

⊘ Does it still need to be done? If not, stop it.

⊘ Am I unquestionably the only person who can do this? If yes, figure out a more efficient way to get it done.

⊘ If someone else in the organization can do it, identify that person and train him or her.

⊘ Can it be outsourced? If so, make it happen.

Focus your attention on a small number of key decisions. CEOs get sidetracked doing all kinds of things, but if you can clear out all the clutter and focus on the two, three, or four decisions that you need to make each year that really matter, you'll be able to dramatically advance the ball in your business.

And remember this: most of what you do can be done better by somebody else. Once you accept that, you'll be able to delegate everything except those few key decisions that make or break your company.

5. Always having to be right

When given a choice between being right and being effective, some CEOs prefer to be right. They don't take others' points of view into consideration, even regarding minor issues. A common misconception about being a strong leader is that they have all the answers. In reality, they do not.

What to do:

Work on developing more patience. It will enhance your interpersonal skills and improve your leadership effectiveness. By getting defensive about your decisions and stopping people in mid-sentence, you also close yourself off to the possibilities of better strategies. Also, when you don't know the answer to something, it's okay. My colleague and good friend Jay Reid says, "The most successful entrepreneurs and CEOs I know are the ones who are constantly asking for input. The ones who seem to struggle the most are the ones who always sit back and think they've got it all figured out." When you do not know something, seek expert guidance.

6. Not enough accountability

You hold your employees accountable for their jobs, but when you make a commitment, who holds you accountable? You may have a board that holds you accountable to certain big items. But who holds you accountable on a day-to-day basis for making sure the key activities that lead to achieving the big items are getting done?

What to do:

Have a mentor or coach hold you responsible for your own goals and actions. The April 2015 *Harvard Business Review* article "CEOs Need Mentors Too" revealed a two-year-long study and found that when CEOs receive mentoring and coaching, good outcomes follow. By clear majorities, the CEOs who received mentoring and coaching said they were:

- ➲ making better decisions

- ➲ fulfilling stakeholder expectations more capably

- ➲ avoiding costly mistakes

- ➲ becoming proficient in their roles more quickly

7. Not putting the right people in the right jobs

This is one of the most common blind spots I see: CEOs don't put the right people in the right jobs because they think their people are going to get better. As hard as it is to say, the people that got you to where you are today typically won't take you to where you want to go tomorrow. This means that as your company grows, you may need to replace longtime employees and hire top-caliber performers who enable your company to jump to a new level.

What to do:

Get the absolute best person for each job. Make sure they fit your culture as I mentioned earlier, using assessments like behaviors/motivators to help you reduce hiring mistakes; pay them well; and if you make a wrong hire, fire quickly.

To help assess cultural fit, my client Nathan Mersereau asks himself a simple question, "Would I want to spend a day in a canoe with this person?" It cuts through the clutter and helps you determine whether this person will be rowing in the same direction as you or whether they are going to rock the boat and tip it over. If they are not canoe compatible, then pass and look for a better hire.

Chuck Davis, a leading CEO, e-commerce pioneer, and past international chairman of YPO, said on our *On Your Mark, Get Set, Grow!* podcast, "There's a big difference from good to great. I think how one hire dictates how one's company performance will end up going." Good employees make for average companies. Great employees spawn unicorns. Take a look at your last five hires. Were they good or great?

8.   Not building a high-performing board

Starting a company or building an existing one to a high level of success requires great people. And these people extend beyond your employees and leadership team. CEOs often neglect the benefit of strategically building a board of directors, investors, informal advisors, and coaches who can move the company well beyond its current trajectory. A strong, well-connected board can give much more than great advice. They can connect you to potential new customers, new suppliers, and new distribution channels that could open up a world of opportunity for you.

What to do:

Take the time to consciously determine who could add great value to your company by being part of your advisory or investor network. Find people with complementary attributes who fill in the gaps you have in your company. Look for highly influential, well-connected people who can open new opportunities for you.

9. Not focusing on your best customers and market segments

In the early days, the focus is on growth. CEOs often take on clients or enter market segments that over time turn out to be black holes. Eventually, your company hits its stride, but you're still stuck with legacy clients or markets that no longer make sense. This can suck the life out of you and your team and take energy away from servicing and pursuing your best opportunities.

What to do:

Identify the specific types of clients and market segments that make the most sense to you. Focus your resources on the highest, best, and most profitable customers and segments and let go of what does not meet that criteria. Sell off part of your business if that makes sense. Perhaps carve out a piece and let some existing employees run with it.

10. Not fully understanding the key drivers of your business

Every business that's growing has a growth engine. Some CEOs look at the top line and take comfort in seeing it rise. Unfortunately, many CEOs don't have a solid grasp on the exact drivers of their growth. They cannot clearly articulate the one or two key activities that drive the business forward. By contrast, the most effective CEOs understand the drivers of that growth and optimize their business to take advantage of it.

What to do:

Take a deep dive on your business model and figure out exactly what drives the growth of your business. And when you determine the growth drivers, develop leading activity metrics to monitor those growth drivers and ensure you are maximizing your opportunities.

11. Not taking advice

CEOs don't make it to the top because they lack confidence. But sometimes this confidence spills over into arrogance and the CEO loses the ability to accept and act on other people's solid advice. I have also seen CEOs who foster a fear-based environment where dissent is quickly squashed. And guess what? When people fear speaking out, they stop sharing their opinion and turn into yes-men and yes-women. Not exactly an environment conducive to stellar growth.

What to do:

Self-awareness is a key here. Be willing to accept advice from trusted and respected advisors and colleagues. Occasionally, you may get bad advice, but the benefits of expanding your brain trust far outweigh the occasional bum advice. Let your team know you want to hear opposing points of view. Create a safe environment where "disagreeing with the boss" is not a one-way ticket to Siberia. Constructive and respectful disagreement is often necessary to reach a better decision. But once the decision is made, everyone must get on board with it.

12.   Not reaching out

It's lonely at the top, and CEOs are sometimes blind to the benefit of reaching out to and networking with other professionals in their same situation. Keeping the pressure and frustrations of being a CEO bottled up inside does not do anybody any good. What's worse is that sometimes these frustrations are taken out on the people closest to us—like our spouses and children.

What to do:

Join one or more organizations that facilitate peer-to-peer connections such as EO, YPO, and Vistage. Regular meetings with peers experiencing the same issues as you will help you grow and reduce your stress. And don't try to be a "tough guy" by holding back and saying, "Everything's fine." If it's not fine, get help.

Embedded in many of these blind spots is the idea that as the CEO, you have to ask great questions, as I mentioned in chapter 6. Great questions and the ensuing answers can lead you to unexpectedly positive results. In fact, I've seen how a single insightful question can completely reframe a problem or an opportunity facing a company and generate a phenomenal result.

My friend Scott Duffy shared a story on our podcast about the time he spent with Virgin founder Richard Branson on Moskito Island in the Caribbean. Branson got a twinkle in his eye and told the assembled group of Virgin executives that he wanted to purchase a rainforest. And not just any rainforest—but the entire Amazon rainforest.

Of course, everyone thought this was impossible. You couldn't possibly buy the Amazon rainforest. But Branson walked the group through an exercise. He simply asked a few questions. First, he asked, "Imagine you wanted to buy the rainforest; how would you do it?" Eventually, he asked, "Do you have to buy the rainforest, *or can you lease it?*" Bam, a light bulb went off.

A simple question about buying versus leasing completely changed the mind-set. Further questioning about using crowdsourcing to allow people of all means to contribute to saving the rainforest suddenly made the attendees realize that buying (or leasing) the Amazon rainforest was not such a far-fetched idea after all. As Scott told me, "Within five minutes, Branson made buying the rainforest sound easier than buying a bowl of soup."

Better questions lead to better answers. As the CEO, you don't have to have all the answers. But in order to *make BIG happen* you do need to ask the right questions.

Chapter 10 Action Steps

☑ Acknowledge that you have blind spots.

☑ Work with your colleagues to identify which blind spots are the most damaging.

☑ Commit to doing whatever is necessary to overcome your blind spots.

CHAPTER 11

Cultivate Healthy Paranoia

Back in the mid-1980s, Intel faced an onslaught of competition from Japanese semiconductor manufacturers. The company was losing millions of dollars on its flagship memory chip business, closing plants and implementing layoffs.

The firm had a big decision to make. Should they slug it out in the fiercely competitive memory chip business or bet the company on the relatively new microprocessor business?

To make this tough decision, senior executive Andy Grove turned to cofounder Gordon Moore and asked, "If we got kicked out and the board brought in a new CEO, what do you think he would do?"

Moore answered without hesitation, "He would get us out of memories." To which Grove responded, "Why shouldn't you and I walk out the door, come back, and do it ourselves?" And that's exactly what they did.

The rest is history. Intel went on to become one of the greatest success stories in business, and Grove ranks as one of the all-time best CEOs.

Grove told this story in his 1996 book, *Only the Paranoid Survive: How to Exploit the Crisis Points That Challenge Every Company and Career.* The idea that "only the paranoid survive" is even more relevant today than it was back then. Why? Because exponential technology is marching across the business landscape and eating slow-moving companies in its path.

Grove's "paranoia" served the company well. Today, Intel is a $130 billion market cap company. All leaders should develop a healthy level of paranoia to keep them sharp and alert for the potential disaster around the corner. And by turning that paranoia into plans, you can overcome any obstacle that may come between you and your goals.

HOPE FOR THE BEST, PREPARE FOR THE WORST

Most leaders find themselves spending the majority of their time reacting to the issues of the day—rather than focusing on where their business is going, how they are going to get there, or what could derail them. Take, for example, a typical executive's day at the office.

You come into work in the morning, stop by the coffee room for a quick hit of caffeine, and spend a little bit of time catching up with a couple of people. Cup in hand, you head back to your office and—first things first—check your e-mail. Many of the messages contain meaningless stuff that has nothing to do with moving your business to the next level. But, being a diligent leader, you want to reply in a timely fashion, so you spend the next hour or two responding. When you're done, you move on to checking your voicemail.

Next comes the line-up at the door, and you begin dealing with the issues of the day. Now it's lunchtime, so you grab a quick bite—or have a non-essential meeting—and come back to the office and repeat the whole process. Before you know it, the day is over and you have gotten a lot of things done; they just weren't the things that will necessarily grow your company or prepare your firm to weather an unexpected event. The items you are processing may be urgent, but they are often unimportant.

In this scenario, you'll never find the time to prepare for the worst, to prepare for the things that could put you out of business.

The fact is, adversity happens, and it happens at some moment to everybody. The question is: When adversity hits, what do you do about it? In the end, it's not so much about what happens but how you deal with what happens. While you cannot predict everything that can go wrong, you can imagine some of the things that can go wrong and plan for them.

When I ask in my speaking gigs how many people have a disaster recovery plan in place, typically, out of a hundred business owners, only four or five raise their hands. That means 95 percent of entrepreneurs are totally unprepared for a potential business-threatening event. So when the building burns down, they don't know ahead of time where everybody is going to work.

You need to get ahead of, rather than behind, those possible business breakdowns. Here's a series of questions I ask my clients to help them prepare for the worst, while they hope for the best.

To begin with, ask yourself, "What are the unplanned events that could put my business at risk?" For example:

- One of your key players on your management team leaves.

- A new government regulation puts your product or service at risk.

- You suffer a product recall.

- A natural disaster occurs.

- Theft of intellectual or real property or staff occurs.

- The health of a key employee is compromised.

- The health of a key employee's family member is compromised.

- Competitors are making your business obsolete.

One big risk I see happening all the time is companies becoming overly dependent on one customer, to the point where if that customer left, the business would be in danger. When I hear that a customer is 30, 40, or 50 percent or more of a client's business, I worry about that company's future. So as a rule of thumb, don't have any customer represent more than 15 percent of your business. If you find yourself in this spot today, start working furiously on diversifying your client base.

Preparing for these business risks is as simple as setting aside time to answer the questions above. Meet with your management team and determine the biggest threats to your business. Then start systematically putting contingency plans in place to prevent them from becoming a business killer if they occur.

CUT EARLY AND CUT DEEP

Not moving fast enough to reduce staff when problems arise is a mistake I've seen companies make—mine included.

When times are tough and companies need to cut overhead, the place they usually begin is with the biggest expense—their staff. The problem is that instead of downsizing in one or two rounds, they do it one person a week for months. This trickle termination leaves the remaining survivors in a panic, wondering, "Am I next?" This can compromise the very survival of the business.

Instead, it is far better to plan your layoffs and execute them all at once, while concurrently informing your staff as to what you are doing and why. Cutting fast, early, and deep is far less painful in the short term and more profitable in the long run. And while most executives I present this idea to nod their heads in agreement and see the logic in this strategy, many are hesitant to employ it.

I felt that reluctance myself during the Wall Street liquidity crisis in 1998, when I laid off 240 of my 275 people at Platinum Capital over one weekend. I had no role for those other thirty-five employees, but I kept them anyway, figuring they were the best of the best and could help us to reinvent ourselves. But in the end, I had to let most of them go as well. It would have been better to have just laid them off with the others rather than continuing to pay them for no purpose other than wishful thinking.

In the mortgage industry collapse of 2007–2008, scores of mortgage, finance, and real estate companies hung on to people even when the handwriting on the wall was clear that they should be cutting expenses to protect themselves. Many of them burned through all their cash and went out of business.

The moral of the story is: if you have to cut, do it early and deep. If you must take the arm off, don't slice one finger at a time; remove the whole arm all at once.

True, you may know these people and their families and not wish to be unkind. You may expect things will get better and in the meantime want to appear strong. But the risk of not doing what needs to be done is that you will jeopardize everybody else left behind. You must consider the greater good. You must have a healthy paranoia about the future and be willing to bite the bullet now for longer-term gain.

INVEST IN TRAINING

In contrast to cutting people, be paranoid about ensuring that your team's skills are top notch.

At Platinum Capital, there were times when our people were in training every day. The goal was to ramp up productivity. We wanted our people to understand every aspect of our products. We wanted them to engage in the most productive sales techniques. We also found that a regular training program was a good way to build company culture.

At our large call center, we trained with our sales team for one hour a day. By doing that over one particular four-month period, we doubled our conversion rate. In other words, if somebody was doing five loans a month, we were able to get them to ten loans a month.

To improve performance, we engaged in role-playing activities. Sometimes the sales staff would argue that the training took away from the precious time that they could be using to sell, but the improvement in results demonstrated the value of the hours spent. They practiced on each other in the training room, with one playing the role of salesperson and another the role of customer. That was far better than trying to hone their skills while making the actual sale—and possibly compromising it.

KEEP YOUR COMPETITORS CLOSE TO YOU

Rather than obsess over your competition, you can develop a healthy paranoia by keeping them close at hand—and it might even net you a new revenue stream.

I was once invited to speak on a conference panel with members of Countrywide, Bear Stearns, and Bank of America. As a result, I not only built relationships with some key players at those institutions, but because of the credibility I gained by being on a panel with them, I was approached by a number of business owners with companies the size of mine who wanted to network and see what we could learn from each other.

I took that opportunity to set up onsite visits with some of those competitors simply by saying, "I'm going to be out your way next month, and I'd love to connect with you the next time I'm in your area. Can I pop in and buy you lunch?" The answer was always yes.

Invariably, when I went by the person's office to pick them up, they would offer me a tour. In one case, as a competitor showed me around the office, he said: "Here's my sub-escrow department." I had never heard that term before, so I asked him, "What's that?" It was a service my competitor offered to title companies that netted him an additional several hundred dollars per transaction.

Shortly afterward, we implemented our own sub-escrow department. Within a year, it had added more than a million dollars to our bottom line.

HAVE ADVISERS CHALLENGE YOUR ASSUMPTIONS

I learned to have my advisers continuously challenge my assumptions. They force me to evaluate the following on a regular basis.

- ❯ Do I have the right plan?

- ❯ Do I have the right vision?

- ❯ Has that vision changed?

- ❯ Am I going to be disrupted?

- ❯ Who is doing it better?

- ❯ Are my key performance indicators the right ones?

- ❯ Am I focusing on the right leading activities, or am I too caught up in the lag measures?

- ❯ Are my key relationships the right ones?

- ❯ Who can help me get closer to them, and how?

- ❯ Are there any new key relationships or strategic partnerships that I should consider?

- ❯ Do I have the right people?

Do you have trusted advisers who can be straight with you? Whether this is your coach, a board of advisors, or a mastermind group, the result is the same—invaluable third-party feedback on your plans.

Like Grove at Intel, a "healthy paranoia" will keep you alert and focused on moving your company forward.

Chapter 11 Action Steps

☑ Have a plan in place to deal with the low-frequency but predictable things that could derail your business. For example, have a disaster-recovery plan, business interruption insurance, and a plan to deal with the loss of a key employee(s).

☑ When faced with having to reduce staff, cut early and cut deep instead of death by a thousand cuts.

☑ Make sure you have outside advisers who can challenge your assumptions and offer perspective that you may be blind to.

CHAPTER 12

Manage through the Roller Coaster

In September 1996, three months after I got married, I signed a lease to move Platinum Capital from our little 6,500-square-foot space to a 24,000-square-foot space. We had about eighty employees at the time, and we were bursting at the seams. The new space would have 160 cubicles. I put a personal guarantee on that lease.

To top off the spending spree, we had just spent more than $200,000 on a marketing campaign.

Then the unthinkable happened.

I worked in our LA office with my business partner, while the best man at my wedding ran the Orange County office. I had stayed out of his way, provided the financing, and let him run that office.

And then one October day, a few weeks after we leased that space, he told me he was leaving. He said he had gotten a dream job on Wall Street, and although he was sad to go it was something he really wanted to do.

It turned out to be a lie.

There was no dream job on Wall Street. He was leaving to set up a competing company two blocks away. And he took most of our people with him. He took all the best salespeople, most of the operating people, and most of the finance people. He took all the receptionists—the phones were ringing incessantly, with no one to answer them. He took our one IT guy. I was left with only new hires and subperformers.

In fact, we were down to twelve people. We ended up moving those dozen souls, plus a few more that we picked up, into our spacious new digs. He left me with a shell of a business, empty offices, a marketing campaign that I could not support, huge financial losses, and a rift that would never heal.

We had been like family. He and his wife had just been over at our home the night before. We were drinking and celebrating success. We were toasting to Platinum Capital. I had seen no sign of his premeditation.

Was I mad? Absolutely. But I chose to fight.

In the rebuilding process, I learned a great deal about myself and how to survive a business catastrophe. I had to dig deep. I convinced Eddie, the top sales guy, to stay, and I think he just felt bad for me. He saw how badly I had been screwed, and he wanted to help. He did an awesome job, and we went on an incredible rebuilding ride together. I sold him my vision, and I kept him on board—and he kept others on board. He helped with the training, and he rallied the people. Additionally, he attracted good hires.

Together, we fought back, we rebuilt—and I learned that life goes on. In a crisis, you can trust your instincts. First, you must believe in yourself. You identify what you can control and what you cannot. I realized that one thing I certainly could control was selling the vision to those who remained and giving them confidence. I reassured them that we would rise again, rebuild, and Make BIG Happen!

FIND ME AN ELEPHANT

"I'm going to show them our vision for this space, for these 160 cubicles, and this whole room where we can expand," I told my assistant. "And so I want you to find me an elephant. A marching band, too. And bring somebody in to tear down the wall to that empty 8,000-square-foot room in the back of the building."

"Mark, you're tired. You've been through a lot lately—" she began, but I gave her a look that spoke volumes. "Okay, a marching band I can understand," she said. "I'll do what I can. But an elephant?"

"Just find me an elephant," I said and went back to business.

She rose to the challenge. On the appointed day, the marching band was there. I rode the elephant down the street and into the annual meeting. We were on the morning and evening news broadcasts. *The Los Angeles Times* and the *Orange County Register* sent reporters. The message was that if you think big and act big, you will be big. We would take this company to a billion dollars, I said. I heard laughter, and I saw tears.

ELEPHANTINE INSPIRATION

STAFF PHOTO/LEE PAYNE

Is it Hannibal? Nope, it's just Moses — Mark Moses, that is, chief executive of the Platinum Capital Group, a mortgage firm in Irvine. He did sort of an imitation of the Carthaginian military leader last Thursday, riding "Kitty" the elephant to his Reynolds Avenue office with the intent of inspiring his troops. Hannibal, it is said, led his army across the Alps with the help of elephants in 218 B.C. to invade what is now Italy.

Irvine World News article on Mark's
famous elephant ride.

By the next day, I was starting to notice an interesting addition to the decor around the office, particularly on people's desks: ceramic elephants, stuffed elephants, and crystal elephants. I felt a clear message: "Hey, pal. We're with you."

From there, we went on a roll. We built the center up to 275 people. Just two years after my best man had departed with most of Platinum's people, we were making more than $1 million a month in net income. We were ranked number ten on the Inc. 500—we were the tenth fastest-growing company in the United States. We won Ernst & Young's Entrepreneur of the Year. I was a finalist for Business Person of the Year in Orange County. We won the Blue Chip Enterprise Award for overcoming adversity. We were gaining recognition as a cool place to work, with an awesome culture. And we were having fun!

Then the music stopped. Again.

In October 1998, as Wall Street was struggling with the Asian flu and the hedge fund crisis, our funders decided to pull out of our industry and abandon our product. It was essentially over a single weekend that we laid off 240 of our 275 people. We kept

Mark and cofounder Brett Dillenberg at the Inc 500 awards conference, and winning the Entrepreneur of the Year.

thirty-five people, figuring they would be part of our rebuilding team. But, in effect, our industry had ended.

For two years, we struggled. All the money that we had made, we lost. We were bleeding $1 million a month. We did all that we could to cut overhead. We stopped our $1 million-a-month marketing program. We cut Bob Villa as our spokesperson. We stopped dropping five million pieces of direct mail a month. It all ended.

"Platinum Loses Its Luster," the *Orange County Register* reported on the front page of its business section in April 2000. It was the lead story and chronicled how this flamboyant company with a cool culture had faded.

It looked bleak. We had borrowed money from family and friends to keep the doors open. We raised $1.5 million, and we were paying 20 percent interest. I had $350,000 in credit card debt. The beautiful home with a lovely ocean view that I had purchased in April 1998, up in the hills in Newport Beach, was now for sale, as was the yacht I purchased after my wedding.

We were trying to reinvent ourselves, but we were coming to realize that we were out of money, and were going to be about $1 million short for our October 13, 2000, payroll. We could see that we weren't going to make it. We hired a bankruptcy lawyer and prepared to file on October 13. My wife was nine months pregnant, and we had an eighteen-month-old. Not the best timing for all of this.

Two days before we planned to file, however, my business partner Brett listened to a speaker who had just sold his business to Sprint for $150 million cash. Brett, a charismatic and charming guy, struck up a conversation with him and told him what we were facing, that we would be going out of business in two days.

"I'll read your business plan on my flight back to Montana tonight," the speaker told Brett. The next day, he emailed us thirty-one tough questions, and we spent several hours on the phone with him answering all of them. He was considering becoming an angel investor for us. "I'll let you know tomorrow," he said—and we figured it had better be tomorrow, since that was the day we would be going out of business. He came back with four more questions. These were pretty easy to answer, and fortunately, he wired the money that afternoon, and it saved the company.

We didn't file bankruptcy—and in fact, from 2000 through 2006, when I exited, we went on a monster roll.

I have no doubt you've experienced a similar roller-coaster ride through your business journey. Bad stuff will happen. But how you respond to these difficult times is what separates an extraordinary leader from an average one.

In the next chapter, I'll share some of the key things CEOs can do to lead effectively during turbulent times.

Chapter 12 Action Steps

☑ Mentally prepare yourself that the good times you may have now could quickly be followed by a significant business setback.

☑ When a business setback happens, you, as the leader, have to step up and give the rest of the team hope that, together, you can all turn it around.

CHAPTER 13

Lead Effectively in Turbulent Times

"Turbulent times." The phrase conjures up a financial slowdown and a tightening credit market. But the economy doesn't need to be in the toilet for your business to go through turmoil.

Even in a booming business environment, your company can still run out of cash, face adverse margin compression, or be threatened by a competitor. Your cost to acquire a customer can become too high, and your marketing can become ineffective. New government regulations could hobble you; you could face a major lawsuit; or you could lose a key staff member, top customer, or main supplier. Your product or service—the reason for your company's existence—could even become obsolete. Any of these can be the reason for turbulent times, even in a growing economy.

Regardless of whether the business environment you are working in today is expanding or contracting, here are some nuggets of advice to help you overcome what's getting in the way of you achieving your goals. There could be an entire book written on this topic alone. Here's a short summary.

COMMUNICATE REGULARLY WITH YOUR TEAM

I was on a flight from Vancouver to Seattle once when the pilot came on the loudspeaker and said, "Flight attendants, grab your seats and sit down now." Just like that—very aggressive and abrupt. Then the plane started to shake, and I swore we were going down.

It was the worst turbulence I have ever been through, and the pilot didn't say one word the entire flight after his initial statement. Not even after we landed. It would have been so simple and yet so powerful for him to tell us what had happened. It was a lost opportunity.

But leaders (like bad pilots) often don't communicate clearly about what is happening and where things are headed—especially in uncertain times. Instead, they lock themselves up with their team behind closed doors to strategize. They become unresponsive, stop returning calls, and do not answer emails, because they are too busy focusing on the problem at hand.

In the meantime, all the people in the organization start making up their own theories and stories about what's going on. And those stories are usually worse than the reality. So now, instead of the staff doing their best work, they are worrying about what's going on in the company and talking about that—over lunch or in the hallways between meetings. And, just like the passengers on a shaky plane, all they want is for their leader to stand up and tell them what is happening.

As my colleague Sheldon Harris said in our *On Your Mark, Get Set, Grow!* podcast, "The more you can push that line out on the edge of transparency and sharing, the more you're going to find employees buying into you, as a leader, into what your company's trying to do, and aligning their efforts with the outcomes you're trying to achieve."

Transparency pays, especially in tough times.

KEEP ATTENDING CONFERENCES

In tough times, when cash is tight, many companies start cutting down their spending on the activities they consider optional. One frequently eliminated item: industry conferences.

On one hand, this makes sense, since the average conference can cost more than $2,500 in registration fees. Add to that hotel, flights, and food, and, if you're taking two or three people, you can quickly find yourself spending in the neighborhood of $10,000. For bigger firms who send twenty or more people and have a booth and display, the cost is much greater. While these types of conferences may have been good for their business in the past, when faced with the realities of a downward economy, companies are hesitant to make that kind of investment.

There's also the timing factor. The executive who just laid off a dozen people may not feel right about going to a conference in Hawaii or West Palm Beach or might simply think, "I just can't be gone right now, given the state of things."

But from my experience, the best of breed still go to conferences, even when cash is tight. They may only send one or two representatives, but they go because they know that networking with their peers and staying on top of the latest and greatest in their fields contributes to building their business.

Smaller companies need to recognize the opportunity that exists at these conferences precisely because fewer people are attending. That gives them a better chance of networking with those key industry players and learning from them. It's also an ideal time to build closer and stronger relationships with the most important customers and vendors—and to learn what peers are doing. I also make it a point to walk the exhibit hall at conferences to see what niches my peers (and vendors) have created. And don't forget to hang out at the bar, since that is where most of the chatter takes place.

What if you want to attend an industry conference and can even swing the expenses but do not feel the attendance fee is within reach? One solution is to offer yourself as a speaker in exchange for free attendance. Frequently, the speakers are representatives from the big guns, so what you might bring to the party would be the small guy's perspective or your specific niche. You could do so as a panelist or as a solo presenter.

Not only can you save on the conference fees, but as a speaker you also gain credibility as a trusted resource. You'll be perceived as someone with industry knowledge or expertise, and other attendees will seek you out for networking. When I used to speak at conferences, I frequently found myself having dinner or drinks with people who had introduced themselves to me after a presentation or with clients and vendors who were impressed that I was on the program. Here are just a few results that came out of those connections:

> ❯ I was often able to get better pricing or negotiate better terms.

- I met competitors from around the country who had different niches than mine.

- I was invited to test new products not yet available to the masses.

- I found new vendors whose niches complemented my core business.

So don't just meet and greet at conferences. Make it a point to visit your competitors on site. What you learn can pay off in better networking and profit.

Over the years, I attended most of my company's industry conferences, YPO's Harvard program for several years to sharpen my axe; the London Business School Program for Entrepreneurship; the Birthing of Giants Program at MIT; and more than a hundred events offered by YPO and EO International. I learned about the importance of meeting other entrepreneurs and business leaders who challenged me to step up my game. One of my most memorable nights was "The Night of the Living Dead" at the Birthing of Giants Program at MIT where we all shared our best and worst business and life experiences. It was a very emotional night with plenty of tears.

TRIM THE FAT

During the good times, companies tend to live off the fat of the land. They take on more overhead—more cost, more perks, more staff. But in turbulent times, they cannot do that. In a tough economy or business cycle, companies must batten down the hatches and examine all of their expenses one by one.

To facilitate this, I have my clients write a list of their ten or fifteen biggest expenses and rate them from the highest (usually staffing) to the lowest. Then I ask them to measure these expenses from month to month, to see where they might be able to cut.

To achieve your cost reduction goals, here are a few ways that my clients have found to cut the fat:

- ❯ If times are tough and you have a manager who is functioning as an overseeing manager, convert that person to a working manager. Then cut the employee he or she was overseeing.

- ❯ Consider what you can outsource domestically or abroad. Many platform-based businesses can do it better and cheaper than you can. Read up on the concepts of the sharing and collaborative economy.

- ❯ Shop bank fees, or, better yet, go with a bank that has none.

- ❯ Go through your third-party expenses, such as telephone, cell phone, delivery expenses, office supply, travel, etc., and find ways to renegotiate the costs or switch vendors.

- ❯ Review all your other vendors and try to negotiate better deals, change vendors, or eliminate the expense altogether.

- ❯ Consider your current space requirements. Are they still what you need, or can you lease out one-third of your building to someone else? Do you need all the offsite storage space you did when the business was growing, or could you bring that storage back in-house to eliminate costs?

- Take a fresh look at all your health plans, insurance policies, and deductibles. Perhaps you have reduced your number of locations and staff and might not need as much coverage. Could you save cash by increasing the size of the deductibles, especially where you seldom file claims?

- Shop payroll companies to see where you can get a better deal.

- Instead of sending everything out overnight, send it second-day. Many of your clients will not notice the difference.

- Consider each and every expense and ask yourself, "Do I really need this, or can I live without it?" When money is tight, it's amazing how people can do without what they had thought were essentials.

You can even do this exercise during good times from a position of strength. By eliminating your bloat, you'll reduce the chance of an outside cost structure taking your company down.

ELIMINATE UNPRODUCTIVE PEOPLE

A long time ago, I read that the bottom 25 percent of salespeople accounted for less than 6 percent of sales. Which led me to wonder, "Why would anybody employ those guys?"

This couldn't possibly be happening in my company, I thought. Just to be sure, I set out to rank all our sales staff based on revenue and gross profit. At the time, I had 160 salespeople, and, as it turned out, our bottom 25 percent only accounted for 3.6 percent of sales and less than 2 percent of gross profit.

Interestingly enough, it was also that bottom 25 percent who turned out to be the ones who complained the most about how unhappy they were with the company. Not only were these people not helping our sales, they weren't doing the company culture any good either, so we let them go.

In working with my own clients and doing this same analysis (ranking sales staff from top to bottom), I've found consistently that the bottom 25 percent often only account for 6 percent of sales or less. Which again brings us to the question, "If these guys are so bad, why do companies keep them?" Here are just some of the reasons I've heard for not eliminating unproductive salespeople or other nonperforming employees:

- ➲ We have already spent a good deal of time, effort, and money to hire and train them. We even spent money on a search firm to bring them onboard.

- ➲ They are likeable people and are friends with other employees.

- ➲ They really need the job, and we don't want to look bad in other employees' eyes by firing them.

- ➲ We haven't really given them enough of a chance.

- ➲ Not everyone can be top of the heap in efficiency, organization, and volume of work.

- ➲ Some people are just not that competitive, but they do a decent job.

- ➲ Not everyone is an "A" player.

In my experience, however, none of those excuses measures up when you consider the damage done by keeping poor performers. To begin with, consider what it's costing you in cash out of pocket to employ them. Typically, they get a base salary in addition to their commission—and often don't earn enough for the company to cover even that. In addition, you are paying for their benefits, the cost of housing them at a desk, their phone, office supplies, etc.

While the money you spend to keep these folks is tangible, the intangible cost is that they are usually the ones whining the loudest about your company. They seem to have a sense of entitlement about what the company owes them in leads, price adjustments, better commissions, and other demands. Underperformers damage overall morale.

So what's the best way to ensure that unproductive staff members don't spoil your success? To begin with, make it company policy that anyone who falls below the 25 percent performer line will be eliminated unless they meet minimum standards of performance. Let every employee know the performance expectations up front. You can give new hires a finite number of months to hit that standard. If they do not, they are gone—and you will not keep carrying them.

Keep in mind that underperforming isn't just about not producing a certain level of sales or specific results; it can also be about making an unacceptable amount of operational mistakes. For example, in the underwriting, processing, and documentation departments of Platinum Capital, we had people who would make a mistake that would cost the company meaningful money. When mistakes were first made, we would sit down with the manager and the entire team monthly for a review. The goal was to help employees learn from one another's mishaps and correct them. Those who did not learn and who kept making the same mistakes were eliminated.

Hanging on too long to employees who are unproductive or culture killers can definitely get in the way of achieving your goals. As I wrote earlier, if they're not working out for you, it's likely not working out for them either. Help them exit your organization so they can move on to another place that is a better fit.

OFFER INCENTIVES

In order to speed up trimming the fat, consider offering incentives.

At one point, I asked my management team at Platinum Capital to come up with a list of cost-cutting ideas. They put some effort into it, but I had hoped for better results. I knew they could do better.

So I went back to them and said, "Look, guys, we need to have greater cuts than you are proposing because we are still operating at a negative cash flow. We've got to resolve this." Then I said I would give them a bonus based on 10 percent of everything they managed to cut.

That's when my managers started to say things like, "Well, I'm managing the department but not doing much of the actual work. I could get rid of three people, have one of my best people step up to do more, and take on some of the work myself. That will eliminate $150,000 in overhead, and I don't think the business will miss a beat." Bottom line: they cut $2 million, and it cost me $200,000.

SELL MORE TO EXISTING CUSTOMERS

For most companies, the lowest-hanging fruit can be found in their existing accounts. Yet most businesses are out there chasing new customers, instead of courting their faithful ones. While it's great to go after new business, in turbulent times it's much easier to sell your stuff to the people who already know, love, and trust you. To begin with, it's important to rank each of your customers. Here is how:

1. Write down the customer's name in one column; then, in a second column, list the gross profit you make from that customer. Gross profit is calculated as sales minus all costs directly related to those sales. For example: your yearly sales from a customer is $1 million, but the cost of sales is $700,000, which makes the gross profit for that customer $300,000. This is the number you would place in the second column.

2. Create a third column and record the gross margin you make from that client. To obtain gross profit margin, divide gross profit by sales. Gross profit margin is expressed as a percentage. For example, if a company receives $1 million in sales and its cost of goods sold is $700,000, then the gross profit margin would be $1,000,000 minus $700,000, divided by $1,000,000, or 30 percent. Basically, a 30 percent gross profit margin means that for every dollar generated in sales, the

company has 30 cents left over to cover basic operating costs and profit.

Whenever I ask people who their best customers are, they usually identify the ones with the highest revenue numbers. But when I dig deeper, I often discover that the highest-revenue customer is not necessarily the most profitable.

3. In a fourth column, record the average order size or average transaction size. The reason for this is that if the margins are the same, you will make more money by selling to the customer with the larger transaction size.

4. In a fifth column, enter the percentage of their business that a customer is giving you. For example, a customer is spending 10 percent of his budget buying from you and 90 percent buying from others like you. I think this is the most important and the sexiest—I call it the gap or share of wallet.

Do this for every one of your customers.

When you take all of the above into consideration, the conversation becomes, "How do I get closer to my most profitable customers so I can close the gap and sell them more of what I have to offer?"

Because you have ranked them in order by profitability and determined the size of the gap (or potential opportunity) that exists, you now know where to focus your efforts for the biggest results. Your job is to create a plan to close that gap and sell more to your best customers.

If you're in a personal services business, such as consulting or financial advising, this strategy is a no-brainer. To start, identify a list of the top 15 percent of your clients as measured by the metrics most appropriate for your business. Then, for each relationship, go through and answer each of the following questions—and write down your answers—don't just "think" about them:

- ❯ What is the status of the relationship?

- ❯ When was the last time you talked to them?

- ❯ When was the last time you met in-person with them and asked engaging questions so you could learn more about who they really are, what their challenges are, and what their dreams are for the future?

- ❯ What is stopping you from making this a better relationship?

- ❯ Who could you introduce them to that could make a difference in their business or life?

- ❯ When was the last time they gave you a referral?

- ❯ When did you last ask for a referral?

- ❯ Who might they be connected to that you would love to have as a new client?

- ❯ What new business opportunities can you pursue with them?

After you've answered these questions, pick up the phone or send an email to each of these people and set a date to meet them for coffee (for your best clients—take them to dinner). Here's where the magic happens. During the meeting, take some time to really get to know your client. Find out how you can do an even better job of making their business or life more rewarding. Find out what they need more help with and connect them to other people as appropriate. It's all about giving at this point.

About halfway through the conversation, start asking for their advice. Let them know you want to continue to improve your business and grow it in a measured way with the right kind of clients (i.e., with people just like them). Ask them how you can improve the experience and results you deliver for them. Ask what they would do differently if they were in your shoes.

Throughout the entire conversation, be open and transparent. The end result is that you'll enrich your relationship, you'll have several new ideas/leads to improve your business and grow your revenue, and your client will have a deeper stake in seeing you succeed since they gave you their advice.

Sounds simple and obvious, right? Most of the businesses I encounter aren't doing this when I first meet them. But most of our current clients now do it, and they have increased their business dramatically by selling more to the customers they already have. It's one quick way to eliminate an issue that could cause stagnant growth in your business.

MAINTAIN YOUR MARKETING BUDGET

When times are tough, many firms start slashing their marketing budget. If you do that, you will be unable to generate more sales. And that's not exactly the antidote to a drop in profits. If everyone else is cutting their marketing budgets, that means fewer dollars are in the marketplace, and you will gain more visibility if you continue your current spend.

I'm not saying spend the money foolishly. I'm just saying that in turbulent times, if you have to cut something, do it somewhere besides your marketing budget. It's what feeds your salespeople to drive more revenue. Additionally, I suggest always allocating a percentage of your marketing budget to testing new ways to generate business.

In their book *Great by Choice*, authors Jim Collins and Morten T. Hansen talk about effective marketing as "firing a bullet." Take an assumption and test it in a low-risk, low-cost way. For those ideas that work, load the cannon and start firing big time. Do not do any "bet the farm" things. Test an assumption, prove it, and then back it with big resources.

This is also a good time to get aggressive with public relations. When times are good, you can pay a PR firm to do the work for you. When money is tight, do it yourself. Brainstorm with your team on some ideas to "create news." There are more media outlets today than ever before and they're all starving for interesting and unusual story ideas.

Earlier, I mentioned how I rode an elephant down the streets of Orange County and right into my office. The image was plastered all over the news. While riding an elephant may not be your thing, there is something you can do to get the media's attention and drive new business to your firm. Make the effort; get the results.

FIND OPPORTUNITY IN ADVERSITY

I learned the importance of finding opportunity in adversity. During troubled times, some of our mortgage competitors were going out of business. It was a great opportunity to hire some of their best people and bring some of their best practices over to our firm. I found that by interviewing these newcomers, they would tell us about some of the special sauce in their previous firms. This became a learning opportunity for us as well.

It is also a great opportunity to acquire firms that might add a profitable product, service, or way of doing business. You could gain some truly accretive financial benefits that could even pay for some or most of the acquisition.

When adversity strikes, it's easy to complain about your situation. And the entrepreneurs and CEOs who fail to rebound from adversity often fail because of how they frame the situation. If they start telling themselves "woe is me" stories, well, you know they are sunk.

On the other hand, if they start asking themselves better questions, they'll find a way to turn the adversity into a victory. These leaders start asking questions such as, "What can I learn from this? Where's the opportunity that this adversity opened up? Where's the stock market equivalent of 'buying low' that's now in front of me? What existing service or product do we have that might be much more valuable to the marketplace in this time of adversity?"

I know, adversity is no fun. I've been there. But I also know if you approach it correctly, adversity will unleash your genius and sow the seeds for your next great success story.

HAVE A DISASTER RECOVERY PLAN

At one of our Platinum Capital monthly meetings, I was standing in front of 150 employees sharing the good news about our spectacular growth and recognizing some of the people who had made a difference.

Partway through the brief pep rally, an explosion shook the building and moments later, a second explosion. The explosions occurred in an electrical room that housed the building's power as well as the server in the phone system. Everyone ran for the doors and across the street.

The fire department rushed to the scene, as did a cadre of reporters. Helicopters were flying overhead. That night, on the evening news, the reporters explained what had happened: An opossum had gotten inside one of the big green service boxes outside the building and had chewed a line.

The city inspectors came out and shook their heads. They told us it would be a couple of months before we would be able to get back to work. Unfortunately, in a couple of months, we would be out of business.

Amid all the drama, while the fire trucks were still on the scene, a guy with a briefcase walked up to me. He was part of an emergency disaster recovery team. "Look, I can help," he said. "Sign these papers, and I can get you back up and running by tomorrow."

The place hadn't burned down, but there was extensive smoke damage. Although I was suspicious, I signed his deal, and he brought in an eighteen-wheeler generator, and he got power back to the building by four o'clock in the morning. The interior was black, smoky, and smelly. The ceiling tiles and insulation had been stripped away.

After a night of drama and uncertainty, good luck, and the help of dozens of emergency disaster recovery workers, we pulled off what seemed impossible. By the next morning, there we were, back at work, in shorts and T-shirts. We had a makeshift server backup and a working phone system.

And in line with our culture of turning negatives into positives and finding ways to bond our team, we greeted employees that morning with a sign that said, "Welcome back! Platinum Capital is on fire … one department at a time!" And the next day, each person got a T-shirt that repeated the slogan, "Platinum Capital is on fire … one department at a time." It was all about culture.

Culture, teamwork, turning negatives into positives; they are an unstoppable combination. Despite the mess and commotion of the explosion, we managed to pull off our best month ever.

I learned three important lessons that day.

First, have a disaster recovery plan. I didn't have one at the time. Leaders anticipate what could go wrong and put plans in place to mitigate the potential damage.

Second, be fully aware of what's in your insurance policies and update them regularly. Investigators determined that the fire was caused by arcing, which the opossum initiated by chewing a line. Sure enough, there was an exclusion in my policy for arcing. I didn't even know what arcing was, yet the damages were over half a million dollars, and the insurance company didn't want to pay.

Third, the fire reinforced the importance of having a positive attitude, despite whatever situation I was dealing with.

DON'T WORRY ABOUT WHAT YOU CAN'T CONTROL

For my own sanity, I learned to not worry about what I cannot control. The weather is uncontrollable, so don't worry about it. The stock market is not controllable, so hire a pro to manage your portfolio and stop worrying about it. Instead, worry about what you do have control over. Don't let things you cannot control keep you awake at night. Save your energy for your team and those closest to you.

If you're still having trouble letting go of your worries, take out a piece of paper and write them down. Then ask yourself, objectively, is this "worry" likely to happen? What's the worst that could happen? How would I overcome if the worst happened? Can I do anything about it? Going through this simple exercise will often expose the worry for what it is—not something you should worry about.

KEEP A GOOD ATTITUDE

Every morning when you get up, you have a choice. You can decide to be one of those guys who moans and groans about how tough things are and go into work with bad body language, looking beaten, or you can go to the office fired up, selling your vision and inspiring confidence as the leader of the band.

That doesn't just mean maintaining a positive attitude. It means facing your problems and figuring out a plan for what it's going to take to resolve them.

Whenever I ask our clients what it's going to take to get out of the current problems they are experiencing, "more sales" is the answer I most often hear. And while, yes, you do need more sales, what you really need are more profitable sales. In other words, gain more business with customers who have higher profit margins and less business with customers who don't. But the real question is: If you want those kinds of sales, how are you going to get them?

Ask yourself: What are the specific activities that it will take to guarantee that we get it done? What's going to stand in the way? How are we going to overcome what's standing in the way? Answer these questions, share the vision with your team, take action, have a system and a process for holding them accountable, and keep score regularly. That's the path to replacing excuses with optimism and ensuring that everyone in your organization sees the glass as half full.

TAKE CARE OF YOURSELF

From a purely physiological point of view, when you exercise you release endorphins and naturally feel good. And when you feel good, you're better able to deal with whatever problems arise in your business.

But what do many folks under pressure start doing? They stop exercising and instead turn to food or booze. They work harder and harder but cannot seem to find the time or motivation to go to the gym because they're so stressed out from the problems at work.

When the liquidity markets collapsed in 1998, I was working my butt off trying to figure out what direction to take the company. I started putting on weight and not eating right. My business coach, Richard Carr, came in for one of our regular meetings and told me that I looked terrible. He asked if I was still working out, and I told him I just didn't have the time or desire. He told me that during the toughest of times it was most critical to keep going to the gym—even if it was only for twenty or thirty minutes. "Just break a sweat, and release those endorphins," he would say. "You'll feel better, and you'll be better able to tackle the challenges that lay ahead." I took his advice, and it always made a difference.

The "too stressed to work out" trap can even effect those who previously had a regular exercise routine in place. Let's say you work out every day at lunch. You come back to the office, you are showered, but your face is still a bit red from all that blood pumping through your system. As you walk through the office with a gym bag slung over your shoulder, your employees see that you have taken the time to exercise.

But what if one day, due to problems in the business, you stop doing that? If you don't think your staff will notice and have a negative interpretation, you're not paying attention. The water cooler conversation will become: "What's going on? The boss stopped working out." Or even worse: "Things must really be bad if he stopped going to the gym at lunch."

Do the exercise that speaks to you. Some of my friends and clients prefer lifting weights or playing basketball; others go for a regular swim or schedule racquetball games. One of my clients dropped twenty pounds and completed the Seattle marathon. My client's new exercise routine increased her confidence and self-esteem and helped her work off a load of stress. She has an ultimate goal of competing in an Ironman, and completing a marathon was her first step. As a bonus, her fitness commitment sent this message to her staff: "You can achieve anything in life as long as you believe in yourself."

You don't need to take up the exercise banner solo. You will inspire employees by inviting them to join you in your exercise goals. I've had clients who did a company sign-up for a local 10K or suggested that team members do a mini-triathlon together. This created wonderful camaraderie for management teams, jazzed up the employees, and, during troubled times, brought groups closer together. The feeling is, "I'm stepping out of my comfort zone and doing something that I may never have done, and my leader is encouraging me to do that."

My client who ran the Seattle Rock and Roll Marathon inspired one of her leadership team members, who wasn't a runner, to do a half-marathon with her. It took almost three and a half hours, and they walked most of it, but their sense of accomplishment in the end was worth it.

For some people, exercising regularly means three times a week. But from what I have seen, they usually end up blowing off one of those days because something comes up. Of course, they say they will make it up on another day—but they never do.

People who build a system and a process to exercise daily are usually able to make it happen. Even if they end up only going to the gym three times a week, that's better than nothing. One final thought: A commitment to meet with a good personal trainer may be the catalyst you need to hold you accountable and get you there.

I've just scratched the surface on possible things you can do to lead effectively during turbulent times. Here's the full list of tips for leading in turbulent times that I address in speaking engagements around the world:

1.   Communicate regularly with your team.

2.   Step away to take quiet time to think.

3.   If you have to cut...cut early and cut deep.

4.   Stay close to your key relationships.

5.   Understand that cash is not cash until it is cash.

6.   Trim the fat...examine all of your expenses one by one.

7.   Incentivize your team to do more with less.

8.   Use technology to drive costs down.

9.   Negotiate better pricing; be Wal-Mart.

10.   Measure everything.

11.   Watch your key indicators.

12.   Eliminate unproductive people.

13.   Invest in training to improve skills.

14.   Try to sell more to existing customers.

15.   Offer incentives for new relationships.

16.   Go to industry conferences and visit your competitors.

17.   Don't slash your marketing budget.

18. There's opportunity in adversity.

19. Have your advisors, mentors, coaches, and forum members challenge your assumptions.

20. Don't worry about what you can't control.

21. Keep a good attitude…look at the glass half full, not half empty.

22. Take care of yourself…exercise regularly.

23. Hope for the best…prepare for the worst.

24. Don't panic…stay steady at the wheel.

25. Make it fun! Culture is always important.

Chapter 13 Action Steps

☑ During tough times, ramp up your communication with your employees, and be honest about the situation but confident in a positive outcome.

☑ Gain some quick momentum by using the strategies described in this chapter to get more business from your existing clients.

☑ Especially during tough times, take care of your health. Regular exercise will help you withstand the pressure of the entrepreneurial roller coaster.

NEXT QUESTION

By now you should be clear on what you want. You know the activities you have to do and the level of thinking necessary to get what you want. You have strategies and plans in place to overcome the inevitable obstacles that can get in the way of achieving your goals. There's only one piece missing to *make BIG happen*— accountability. What's going to ensure you follow through? That's our focus for Question 4.

QUESTION 4

CHAPTER 14

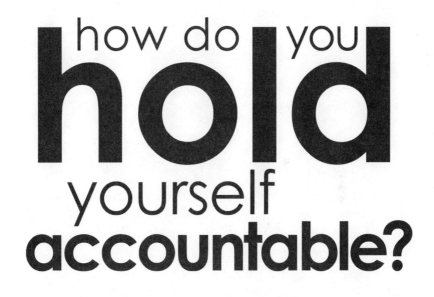

Keep Score

Imagine going to a hockey game. You're sitting in the arena as the home team takes the ice. Music is blasting. The crowd is pumped. And then, seconds before the referee is ready to drop the puck, the scoreboard goes blank.

The announcer comes on the loudspeaker and says, "Sorry, we'll try to get the scoreboard fixed, but in the mean time, we're going to play and keep score at the referee's table."

Do you think that would kill some of the enthusiasm in the arena?

It's no different in business. You need to create a compelling scoreboard to monitor all your key indicators.

Already tracking your results? Probably not the way I'm suggesting.

Often, companies track results, but only the management team sees them. That won't help the folks on the front line who are interacting with your clients on a day-to-day basis.

We coach our clients to create visually appealing scoreboards and post them around the office so everybody can see them. You can be creative and use bar charts, line graphs, trend lines, thermometers, or whatever format works for you. Some of our clients simply use an Excel spreadsheet as their scoreboard.

Here are some things to keep in mind when developing your scoreboard:

1. **It should be highly visible.** All employees should have easy access to it and be exposed to it everyday.

2. **It should be easy to understand.** With one simple glance, employees should be able to tell how the firm is doing. No interpretation necessary.

3. **It should be updated frequently.** Stale data does not inspire anybody, so keep it updated as frequently as daily.

4. **It should display all of the key indicators for which you are trying to drive results.** This includes HOTs, leading activities, and your lag measures.

Depending on the size of your company, you may have one or more scoreboards. Smaller companies may have just one company-wide scoreboard that the entire team is focused on. Larger companies may have multiple scoreboards, perhaps specific to each department.

If you have multiple scoreboards, the items you track on each scoreboard must ultimately be aligned with and support achieving your company's overall HOTs.

As you can see, it's critical to set the appropriate HOTs because those will filter down your company to the departmental level. If you set the wrong HOTs, your team will work hard, but you'll end up in the wrong place.

Knowing what you have to do to "win" is a key benefit of the scoreboard. I mentioned earlier that your scoreboard should show your HOTs, leading activities, and lagging indicators. By watching how progress on your leading activities moves the needle on your lagging indicator results, your team will stay enthused and focused on doing what's necessary to hit your numbers.

Let me digress for a minute to make another point.

I have some clients who are financial advisors. Over the years, I've become pretty familiar with the type of advice they give to clients. One thing I've noticed is sometimes the advice they give is not "mathematically correct."

Now, before you start making snarky jokes, let me give you an example of what I mean.

Let's say an advisor's client is trying to climb their way out of debt. One advisor might recommend the client focus on paying down the highest interest rate debt first—even if it's the largest debt balance. This would be "mathematically correct" because you will save the most interest.

Another advisor might recommend paying off the *smallest balances first*. Why? It's psychological. By getting "small victories" and knocking off these small debts one after another, the client might be more motivated to keep at their debt-paying strategy. By contrast, if the client started on the highest interest rate debt first, they might become discouraged at their lack of progress and go back to their harmful spending habits.

The scoreboard works in a similar fashion to the "small victories" idea.

By tracking your results and seeing progress on a regular basis, your team will stay motivated, engaged, and on track. I've seen it happen over and over with my clients. It can happen in your company, too.

Remember the hockey game. People will pay attention when they know the score ... and when they have a chance to win.

MONITOR THE APPROPRIATE KEY PERFORMANCE INDICATORS (KPIS)

How do you know if your business is performing well? Sure, you can look at sales and profit numbers, but the best CEOs go much deeper and create KPIs that cut to the heart of what makes their business tick.

Here are three criteria to use when developing your KPIs:

1. They must be based on the company's goals.

2. They must be based on activities that are critical drivers of the company's success.

3. They must be mathematically measurable.

Key performance indicators will help you spot problems before they become big issues. Here are three examples of KPIs and how you can use them.

1. Accounts receivable turnover = net credit sales/average accounts receivable

This ratio measures how well you are turning accounts receivable into cash. Higher numbers improve your cash flow and liquidity. For example, if your ratio is three, it means you collect your average accounts receivable balance every four months.

If this number is declining, it's time to have a daily meeting with your team to assign action items and accountability. Pay attention to accounts receivable turnover for thirty to sixty days with a daily meeting, and you will solve your cash flow problems. Clients Norm Curtis from Keystone Western in Winnipeg, Canada, and Sheldon Wolitski from the Select Group in Raleigh, North Carolina, did this and made substantial improvements in their cash flow.

2. Gross profit margin = (revenue – cost of goods sold)/revenue

Gross profit margin helps you monitor your costs and your ability to pass along price increase. It gives you a sense for whether your costs are too high, your prices too low, and the overall competitive strength of your company.

If your gross margin is falling, take immediate action. Client David Thornhill from Integrated Textile Solutions solved his falling gross margin problem in four steps. First, he recognized it by having a KPI. Second, he raised prices. Third, he shopped vendors for better pricing. And fourth, he increased the productivity of the people in the plant by measuring their progress and reducing waste on inventory. Client Tim Kreytak at Ironside, a professional services firm, meaningfully improved his gross margin by increasing utilization of his consultants from around 60 percent to over 80 percent.

3. Customer acquisition cost = total sales and marketing costs in period n/ new customers in period n

This key number tells you how much you have to invest in sales and marketing to bring in one new customer. A rising number indicates your cost to bring in a new client is rising—and that's not good.

If you have a problem here, there are numerous areas to examine. Look at your sales team. Have you noticed any drop in efficiency? Perhaps it's time to hire a new VP of sales, invest in more training and role-playing, set minimum standards of performance, or apply peer pressure by posting everyone's results and cut the bottom 25 percent. How about your email marketing campaign? Are open rates and conversions declining? Are you doing A/B testing on your campaigns?

As in a hockey game, keeping score and monitoring your KPIs will go a long way to ensuring that you end up on the winning side.

Chapter 14 Action Steps

☑ Develop a scorecard to track progress toward your HOTs and make it highly visible throughout the company.

☑ Identify and track key performance indicators to add more context to the progress you're making toward your HOTs.

CHAPTER 15

Hold Regular Accountability Meetings

The last thing anybody wants is another meeting to fill the calendar. Believe me, I hate meetings as much as the next guy. But I've learned that the right meetings are worth the time.

Meetings where strategies and tactics are hashed out and agreed upon are worth your time. Meetings where each team member is held accountable for what they said they would do are worth your time. Meetings to recognize employees and keep the lines of communication open are worth your time.

Short of that, well, you have better things to do.

In chapter 1, I described a communication calendar I've used successfully for many years. It consists of the following:

1. An annual state of the company address

2. A quarterly planning session with the leadership team

3. A monthly leadership team update to its staff

4. A weekly working session with the leadership team

5. A daily huddle with each management team

Now, let's add an annual strategic planning meeting to the list followed by some additional thoughts on the daily huddle.

STRATEGIC PLANNING MEETING

You've probably heard the saying, "Culture eats strategy for breakfast." It's the idea that in companies with established cultures, it's hard to succeed with a strategy that isn't aligned with the existing culture—or close to it.

If your firm is still young, the culture may not have firmed up yet, so you can use your strategies to help shape the culture. If your culture is already embedded, then strategy should, for the most part, work with your existing culture.

I've learned from facilitating more than 250 strategic planning sessions over the past twenty years that culture is one of many things that can trip up even the best-laid strategic plans.

When CEOs ask me whether they should facilitate their own annual and quarterly planning sessions or whether they should get an outside facilitator to do it, I always say, "Go with an outside expert."

By having an outside facilitator, the CEO can participate rather than have to run the show. He or she will be less likely to unduly influence the others who might feel intimidated or simply fall in line with the direction the boss wants to go.

Here's the process we use when I facilitate strategy sessions for clients. Pretend that you're one of our clients:

1. Each participant will receive a strategy workbook in advance. The workbook contains a series of questions we will lead you through on strategy day.

2. Typically, we begin by asking, "What do you want to get out of the day?" Often, we hear the same thing. You want to know where the company is headed, who is responsible for what, and you want the team to be aligned and unified.

3. Then we will step you through a twelve-month review (for an annual strategy meeting) or a three-month review (for quarterly meetings). We will ask you to answer these three questions:

    1. What went right over the last twelve months?

    2. What went wrong?

    3. What did we learn?

4. Next, we'll identify the opportunities and threats/challenges that lie ahead. There's usually no shortage here.

5. After exploring opportunities and threats, we'll gaze into the "crystal ball." This is an exercise where we look at the

year ahead. If it's January, we will ask you to imagine it is December 31. In the first step of the exercise, you will respond to the following: "Describe the year ahead of you based on the crystal ball's prediction. The year has come and gone and we 'rocked' because we achieved the following specific and measurable outcomes." You'll then list several of those achievements that would have made it a fabulous year.

6. The second step of the crystal ball exercise is where the rubber meets the road. We will ask you: "What are the top five things ranked in order that are specific and measurable that made it such a great year?" These are the activities that led to the result in question one. Most people really struggle with step 2 on the specifics.

7. Then we'll ask you those three provocative questions I discussed earlier. We'll set the scenario by asking you to imagine you are starting a new company to compete with your current company. Then come the three questions: (1) What would you stop doing that you are doing now? (2) What would you start doing that you aren't doing now? (3) What would your new company do to try to put your current company out of business?

8. By now, you'll be really warmed up and we'll take a look at some longer-term planning issues by delving into these questions.

1.   Where do we want to be three years from now?

2.   What will it take to guarantee we make it happen?

3.   What will stand in the way of making it happen?

4.   How will we overcome what stands in the way?

9.   Based on the answers from above, we'll develop HOTs, as discussed in chapter 2. I recommend a small number of HOTs at the corporate level, but, depending on the size of your company, each team or department may have their own HOTs that support the corporate HOTs.

10. Then we'll have you identify the top five initiatives that will enable each of those goals to be met. For example, let's say HOT number one was to grow sales by $10 million. The first initiative might be to hire five salespeople who can each sell $2 million apiece. Then, we'll ask you the following questions about each initiative:

1.   What will it take to guarantee it happens?

2.   What will stand in the way of making it happen?

3.   How will we overcome what stands in the way?

4.   Who owns it?

5.   When will it be done?

6.   How will we keep score?

11.   For the next step, we will recommend you take each initiative and rank them in order. Let's say you have four goals, each with five initiatives. That makes twenty initiatives. Rank them in order. You will find that some of those will be combined. Some of them won't feel as important anymore. In the end, you'll probably have eight to twelve initiatives as a company.

12.   Next, we'll turn the spotlight to each of you attending and pose these two questions. You should answer them in an honest self-assessment.

    1.   What should I start doing to get the most out of my own performance and when?

    2.   What should I stop doing and when?

13.   We will end with a section on action steps (next steps), including who is the "owner" of each step, and set a due date for when it will be completed. These action steps help ensure what you learn in the day's session will be modeled and communicated.

It's a long day but a good one. And while strategy sessions are serious business, you can also use them for team building.

For one of our quarterly planning sessions with my client Grasshopper, the entire management team went to Cozumel, Mexico. We did a half Ironman down there, and it was a powerful bonding experience. We had a monsoon that day, so we were running in ankle-deep water. Because the team building was so strong, it was probably my favorite quarterly event that we've ever done with any client. We shared a house. We experienced it all together, and we still tell stories about it.

Mark in Cozumel, Mexico, with the management
team from Grasshopper.

THE DAILY HUDDLE

Being frequently interrupted throughout the day kills your productivity. Sure, you want to have an "open door" policy, but there are better ways to be accessible while still maintaining a high level of productivity.

You may have heard of it. It's called the daily huddle.

Each day, get your team together for a brief meeting. And when I say brief, I mean it. Ten minutes is about right. Start on time. Have a facilitator. Quickly share something positive; it could be personal or business. Ask a question if you need something answered, share the biggest item you will be focusing on today, the biggest challenge you are facing or how you will make a meaningful impact today. Just get it all out so you can get on with your day.

By quickly checking in with your team on a daily basis, you'll forge deeper bonds, eliminate most of your daily interruptions, and stop potential problems in their tracks. And here's a quick tip—do them standing up.

CULTURE OF ACCOUNTABILITY

The series of meetings I've outlined from the daily huddle to the annual strategic planning meeting are critical to ensuring the success of your company. Why? Because they embed a culture of accountability throughout the organization.

There's no place to hide. When you meet daily and report on your HOTs weekly, you and your team have to perform. And yes, this puts pressure on each team member to get the job done.

Keep in mind, there's good pressure and bad pressure. Bad pressure is like Enron. You're so focused on hitting the numbers that you'll cut corners—and break the law—to meet management goals. Good pressure walks the fine line between just enough to compel top performance and not too much to encourage bad behavior.

Your culture plays a dramatic role in how the pressure to perform is perceived. If you've built a fear-based culture where people are penalized or fired for failure, well, you know what will happen.

Think like a sports coach here. They'll yell and scream at a player for making a dumb move one minute, then the next they'll give them a bear hug for a great play. While I don't recommend yelling and screaming, you get the idea. Be firm in reviewing mistakes or shortfalls but lavish praise, too, when appropriate. As long as your team knows that your number-one objective is to help them get better, they'll perform and take the constructive feedback for what it is—your sincere desire to help them.

Top basketball coach Rick Pitino said, "The key is not getting people to work hard. The key is to get them to like working hard." Good leadership and the right culture will do that.

LEVERAGE A COACH

The most successful entrepreneurs and CEOs have found a way to benefit from the concept of leverage. They leverage people by hiring great talent. They leverage technology by strategically implementing the right tools. And they leverage coaches by tapping their wisdom and their ability to instill accountability.

I'm not going to give you a hard pitch here to hire a coach. I just want to share three thoughts for you to keep in mind.

First, nobody has all the answers. The top entrepreneurs and CEOs, while full of confidence, are smart enough to know they don't know everything. You cannot possibly be an expert in every facet of building and running a great company. But you certainly have the smarts to know what you don't know. Like the librarian who points patrons to specific books, you can turn to coaches and other experts whose expertise complements yours.

Second, when you have to answer to someone, you answer. If you join a gym, it's easy to justify sleeping in on a cold morning. But if you're paying a personal trainer whether you show up or not, chances are you're going to get your butt out of bed and make it to the gym. Coaching is no different. When someone is expecting you, you will show up. You will do the work. You will be held accountable and you won't disappoint. That's just your personality.

Third, I eat my own cooking. I have had coaches since I played tennis seven days a week in high school. I played squash in my twenties. I took up golf in my thirties and triathlon in my forties. I had coaches for all of these activities, sometimes multiple coaches. I had a swim coach, a cycling coach, and a personal trainer. On the business side, I have been coached since I was twenty-four. To excel, I needed someone to push me, to challenge me, to force me out of my comfort zone. Coaches serve that role.

I'm a great example that coaching works. Whether it's business or personal, my results have improved measurably by working with a coach. In my company, we have concrete statistics on the average revenue and profit growth achieved by our clients. You can visit www.ceocoachinginternational.com/coaching for the latest numbers.

It does not come as a surprise that entrepreneurs and CEOs aren't the easiest coaching candidates. But ask anyone who has experience with CEO coaching, and they will tell you the experience has been transformative, both for their businesses and themselves.

So if the benefits are great, how do you become coachable? Here are four keys:

1. Be Connected.

Ask for recommendations from executives and business owners who have been coached. Find someone who is an expert in the areas where you or your company is struggling. Find somebody that resonates with you.

2. Be Vulnerable.

Many CEOs are concerned about losing themselves or their company direction as a result of too much external advice. But keep an open mind and realize this is a new experience that may be out of your comfort zone.

3. Be Curious.

Ask lots of questions in regards to your issues and the coach's experiences. They have likely been there before or have seen the issues several times with others.

4. Be Committed.

If you think you cannot afford the time away from the business, remember that meetings with your coach can range from weekly to monthly to periodically, based on need. Give yourself six to twelve months as a tryout period. The investment is often less than the cost of an executive assistant.

Whether you work with us or another coach, the key is to find one who you respect and who has measurable results.

Chapter 15 Action Steps

☑ Implement an annual strategic planning meeting with regular follow-ups. Use a third-party facilitator.

☑ Use the series of daily, weekly, quarterly, annual, and strategic planning meetings to develop a culture of performance and accountability.

☑ Consider hiring a coach who can provide outside perspective, expertise, and additional accountability.

CHAPTER 16

Use Accountability Mechanisms

You have a communication plan in place, which spans from the daily huddle to the annual strategic planning meeting. You're benefiting from the wisdom of a coach and the accountability they instill. What's missing are the tactical moves you can make to ensure your day is productive and your operations run smoothly.

PUT SYSTEMS IN PLACE

Whether we're talking business or personal, my life is filled with systems—and they work.

A system is a formalized mechanism that helps to ensure that you perform an activity according to a certain standard. For example, it could be a ritual that you perform every morning to prepare for your day. It could be a written procedure that details exactly how to perform a certain task. Or it could be a checklist that outlines the specific steps necessary to complete an activity.

Let's use a checklist as an example. After all the training and preparation, there's one thing I'm obsessive about on Ironman race day: my pre-race checklist. I break it down into sections and include everything I need for each aspect of the event. I account for the items that need to go into my transition bags, the food that I plan to eat the morning of the race, and everything I need to do when I arrive at the race site in the morning. I take this list to the transition area with me and review everything one more time.

You may be thinking this is overkill, but invariably I hear an announcement like this at a race: "If anyone has an extra helmet, goggles, or wetsuit, we have a racer who forgot his this morning." Without my Ironman pre-race checklist, I would not be able to finish the race. It gives me the confidence to know that I have everything that I need, and this, in turn, reduces race anxiety.

Think about your work. Have you ever arrived at an important meeting only to find that you forgot the power cord to your laptop? Or didn't have a printed backup of your presentation when the projector malfunctioned?

Which aspects of your business could benefit from a checklist? Discuss them at your next daily huddle. Get the team working on them. Checklists can save your skin. I know; they've saved mine.

MAKE CONSISTENT INCREMENTAL IMPROVEMENTS

In business, it's often a winner-take-all scenario. Either you get the business or you don't. But what if just a few small improvements, compounded over time, could lead to more business and big profits? Would you work on those small improvements? Sure you would. Let me give you an example Steve Sanduski shared with me from the world of golf.

In 2015, Phil Mickelson earned $51 million split between prize money on the tour and endorsements. His per-round stroke average was 70.5. By contrast, ever heard of Roger Sloan? Me either. Sloan won $133,000 on the tour. I couldn't find anything he endorsed. His per round stroke average was 72.5.

You see where this is going?

Mickelson bested Sloan by an average of just two strokes per round yet Mickelson earned *383 times more money*. In other words, Mickelson was just 2.8 percent better than Sloan, but that small margin added up to an extra $50 million in Lefty's pocket.

Just think, one missed putt or one wayward tee shot every nine holes made the difference between being the world's thirty-sixth highest paid celebrity and total obscurity. It's the same in business. Small mistakes could cost you millions.

Make a point to identify areas of your business where consistent, 2.8 percent improvements compounded over time could *make BIG happen*. Here are a few to get your started:

- ➲ Increase response rates by 2.8 percent.

- ➲ Increase quality leads by 2.8 percent.

- ➲ Increase conversions by 2.8 percent.

- ➲ Increase referrals by 2.8 percent.

- ➲ Increase average sales price by 2.8 percent.

- ➲ Increase average profit margin by 2.8 percent.

- → Increase productivity by 2.8 percent.

- → Increase inventory turnover by 2.8 percent.

- → Reduce costs by 2.8 percent.

Make small improvements. Rinse, repeat. It's a simple formula that works.

ASK ACCOUNTABILITY QUESTIONS

In chapter 6, I discussed the importance of asking better questions. You can also use questions as an accountability tool. By asking the right questions, you can hold yourself (and your team) accountable for making better decisions.

For example, as a leader, you have to make tough decisions. But do you have any specific framework for making those decisions? My former client and now colleague Sheldon Harris says leaders should ask the following two questions before making a crucial decision:

1. What's the worst-case scenario if this doesn't work?

2. If it's a decision related to a competitor, ask, "How would I feel if my competitor made this decision and got there before me?"

I often find that key decisions get analyzed to death for fear of making the wrong decision. But if you answer question one above, you'll often find the worst-case scenario is not that bad. My advice is that it's better to make a decision quicker and adjust over time as needed than to delay a decision while gathering more facts. The world moves too fast today, and leaders who are slow to decide will fail.

TEST AND MEASURE

I'm a firm believer in the idea of thinking big, starting small, and scaling fast. Thanks to today's technology, it's so much less expensive to start a new company or launch a new product today than it was just ten years ago. If you couple the lower cost with a test and measurement mind-set, you have a formula for business success.

Earlier, I mentioned the idea of "firing bullets." You come up with an idea or hypothesis. You test it in the marketplace. You analyze the results. Then you adjust as needed, and when you have a winner, go big with it.

My client Grasshopper was a master at this test-and-measure idea. On our podcast, Grasshopper chief operating officer Don Schiavone said in the early days of the company, they would set a growth target but they had no reliable way to know which strategy or tactic would lead to hitting the number.

Today, they come up with multiple growth ideas, carefully test and measure the results of each one (fire bullets), then fully back those ideas that generate the best results. Without a rigorous testing mind-set like this, you're simply stabbing in the dark.

I apply this test and measurement idea to my athletic performance and workouts with the same discipline that I apply to my business. Every workout I do gets entered into my training log. I track the number of yards that I swim, the miles I bike and run, my interval splits, heart rate, cadence, power, calorie intake, fluid intake, salt tabs consumed, etc. Each week, I review the data with my coach, compare it to prior weeks' activities and use it to determine my workout needs for the upcoming weeks.

From years of testing and measuring in my triathlon training, I know that on the bike portion of an Ironman, I need to consume three hundred calories every hour, drink an additional bottle of water when it's really hot, and take four to eight salt tablets per hour depending on the heat. On the run, I need to consume 150 calories per hour and take in approximately twenty ounces of water. This means that at times, I need to drink when I'm not thirsty, eat when I'm not hungry, and take salt tablets even if I'm not sweating much. I know I will suffer later on if I deviate from the plan.

As I said earlier, "If you can't define it, you can't measure it. If you can't measure it, you can't manage it." So whether we are talking business testing and measuring like Grasshopper or athletic performance like my Ironmans, if you instill a test and measure mind-set throughout your organization, you'll dramatically improve your results.

GET MORE DONE

Like you, I work hard. But given a choice, I'd rather get more done in less time. My daily schedule is structured to do that. Here's what it looks like:

- Wake at 4:50 a.m.

- Between 5:00 a.m. and 5:40 a.m., review the day's priorities; read updates from clients that came in over night; and review and make posts on Linkedin, Twitter, and Facebook.

- Head to the gym at 5:40 a.m. and workout until 8:00 a.m.

- Stop at Starbucks on the way home for a grande coconut milk latte.

- Between 9:00 a.m. and 10:00 a.m., prepare for calls.

- Work straight through between 10:00 a.m. and 4:00 p.m., with coaching calls and other activities.

- Before leaving the office for the day, rank in order everything that needs to get done the following day, review follow-up notes from two assistants, clear email, and be 100 percent caught up by 5:00 p.m.

- Have dinner with my family, enjoy a glass of red wine on the deck at sunset, head to bed at 8:30 p.m., watch the news, then lights out by 9:00 p.m.

As just mentioned, I'm meticulous in tracking my activities. I track my workouts through an app called TrainingPeaks. I track vacation days versus business days and don't travel more than thirty days per year for business. I plan on one hundred days of family travel per year.

I track my personal, fitness, and business goals and meet each year for a full day with my accountability partner, who holds me accountable. And in my business, I track a wide variety of metrics and review them frequently with my partners.

And it's not just me who's focused on getting things done. At the dawn of every New Year, everyone in my family posts on the refrigerator their goals for the year ahead. Every Sunday, we have a family meeting and we take turns running it. I want my children to learn those traits of goal setting, vision, communication, confidence, and accountability, too.

Some might say I'm a creature of habit. I place everything in the same place every time. Keys, sunglasses, phone, iPod, and a host of other things each have their place. I'm not going to waste time trying to hunt something down.

I don't forget things when traveling, because I follow a travel checklist. I use Tripit to organize my travel documents.

Great ideas get written down. I keep a pad of paper and pen in the bedroom and bathroom in case something hits me.

Little things don't bog me down. I happily delegate everything I can. I couldn't tell you where the light bulbs are in my house. I don't move big objects, and if it involves using my hands, it's outsourced.

This structure works for me. It may not work for you. Either way, you have to find a rhythm and level of structure that enables you to work at your most efficient and highest level to get more done.

Here are a few more ideas on how you can get more done:

1. **Work from a prioritized daily to-do list.** Each day, write down what you need to accomplish that day, in order of priority. Ideally, these are the things that move you toward achieving your HOTs.

2. **Time block.** Set a specific amount of time to accomplish the important items. Constraining your time will force you to stay focused and get it done.

3. **Remove distractions.** When you're hunkered down, let your assistant know not to interrupt you. Don't look at email. Let the phone go to voicemail.

4. **Stop multi-tasking.** Contrary to popular belief, multi-tasking leads to lower productivity and less-than-stellar work. Stop it.

5. **Take five.** Every hour or so, take five minutes to stretch, get a drink, or go for a walk. Brief breaks will allow you to return to work with more energy and focus.

Peter Drucker said, "Efficiency is doing things right; effectiveness is doing the right things." There's nothing worse than optimizing something that shouldn't be done at all. So above all, when trying to get more done, make sure you're doing the right things.

Chapter 16 Action Steps

☑ Implement accountability mechanisms, such as checklists and systems and procedures.

☑ Focus on making consistent, incremental improvements day after day.

☑ Be fanatical about testing and measuring everything—and then adjust as needed.

☑ Pay close attention to your level of productivity, and use the best practices described in this chapter to stay focused on your highest and best use.

NEXT STEP

You now know The Make Big Happen Questions. You've heard many examples of how our clients and I have put these questions into practice and built dozens of multimillion-dollar companies. I've shared numerous success stories. Now it's time to pull it all together.

Develop a Plan and Commit to Make BIG Happen!

There are three kinds of people: those who make things happen, those who let things happen, and those who ask, "What happened?" This book, of course, is for those who make things happen.

The Make Big Happen Questions are your roadmap to success. You can apply them in any endeavor, whether it is personal, health, or business.

1.   What do you want?
2.   What do you have to do?
3.   What could get in the way?
4.   How do you hold yourself accountable?

I encourage you to make an appointment with yourself and go through these questions three times. Answer them for your personal life, your health, and your business, in that order.

As you approach these questions, it's critical that you start with the right mind-set. Forget your past baggage. Let go of your limiting beliefs. Part ways with the stories you've told yourself that are holding you back. As a kid from a no-name town in Canada who's endured his share of setbacks yet risen above them, I can assure you that success—however you define it—is within your reach.

Start with your personal life. What do you want? Let's assume, for example, you want a better relationship with your spouse. Then ask yourself, what do you have to do to make that happen? I'll bet you already know the answer. It's not rocket science.

Now, what could get in the way of improving your relationship? Maybe you're working too much and not making your spouse a priority. Perhaps the flame has died and you're just not making an effort to rekindle it. Simply acknowledging what's getting in the way is a big step forward.

To come full circle, you have to decide how you're going to hold yourself accountable to improving your relationship. If working too much is a problem, you might restructure your work schedule. For example, start small. You could decide you'll be home by 6 p.m. on Wednesdays and Fridays to share dinner with your family. Make that an unbreakable appointment on your calendar. Have your spouse text you at 5:30 p.m. if you need a reminder.

Once you complete this for your personal life, repeat the process for your health.

Let's take a deeper look at how this process applies to your business by going through The Make Big Happen Questions.

WHAT DO YOU WANT?

As the leader, you must clearly articulate where you're heading and why you're heading there. You must set the bar high and create an environment that compels your team to jump higher, run faster, and throw farther than they have ever done before.

Take time to develop a compelling vision for your company's future. Spread that vision throughout the company. To put meat on the vision, develop one or two Huge Outrageous Targets (HOTs) that, when met, will transform your company and keep it on a path toward the vision.

To track progress on your HOTs, implement a formal set of accountability and planning meetings, including daily, weekly, monthly, quarterly, and annual. Bring in an outside facilitator to run your strategic planning meeting.

Once you know what you want, you have to determine what you have to do to get it.

WHAT DO YOU HAVE TO DO?

Here's where many entrepreneurs and CEOs get tripped up. They have a good idea of what they want to accomplish by setting

HOTs. But they don't develop the right leading activities that, when accomplished, will guarantee the HOTs are met.

The key is to identify the leading activities that will lead to achieving the HOTs. Conceptually, it's easy to understand. The trick is to keep digging until you are certain that the leading activities you identified will, without a doubt, lead to achieving your HOTs.

Once you've identified these leading activities, develop metrics to track your progress on executing the leading activities (lead measures) and metrics to track the result of your execution (lag measures).

And as the CEO, don't get lost in the weeds. Focus on the five important things you should spend your time on: vision, cash, people, key relationships, and continuous learning.

While you're busy "doing," you must also have a plan to overcome whatever could get in the way of achieving your HOTs.

WHAT COULD GET IN THE WAY?

Stuff happens, so you need a plan to deal with the low-frequency but predictable things that could derail your business. For example, have a disaster recovery plan, business interruption insurance, and a plan to deal with the loss of a key employee(s).

You, of course, could get in the way, too. Acknowledge that you have blind spots. Work with your colleagues to identify what they are, and then commit to doing whatever is necessary to overcome them. Make sure you have outside advisers who can call B.S. on you and stop any destructive issues dead in their tracks.

Mentally prepare yourself now, from a position of strength, that the good times could quickly be followed by a significant business setback. And when the setback happens, you, as the leader, must step up. You have to be the one who rallies the team, who gives them hope, who shows them a path to a bright future.

Finally, you have to make sure things happen.

HOW DO YOU HOLD YOURSELF ACCOUNTABLE?

I've found that most people are not capable of holding themselves accountable for following through. You may have the best intentions, but when push comes to shove, most people cannot rely on self-discipline and their own "smarts" to get them to where they want to go.

As humans, we perform better when we have someone else who takes an interest in our success. Whether you call it a coach, an accountability partner, a mentor, or a friend—the outcome is the same. We get better results when we work in partnership with other people.

If you don't already have this "someone" who takes an interest in your success, who can share their wisdom and hold you accountable, then go out and find them. In your personal life, it may be your best friend. For your health, a personal trainer will fit the bill. And in business, a coach is the common solution.

GO FORWARD

By answering these questions and finding people to help hold you accountable, you'll be in an exclusive group of achievers who have taken the time to consciously and proactively decide what they want out of life.

I know it's not easy. Few people have taken the time to really get clear on what they want out of life. But you're different. You're reading this book. You're making the effort to put these ideas into practice. And your efforts will be rewarded. I can assure you of that.

Now go forward and *make BIG happen!*

A Personal Story

One October day in 2004, a day that was much like many others as I swam in the swirl of family and entrepreneurial life, our three-year-old son Mason complained of a headache. Soon he was vomiting.

One thing led to another and, before long, my wife and I stood in disbelief as the doctor told us Mason had a brain tumor.

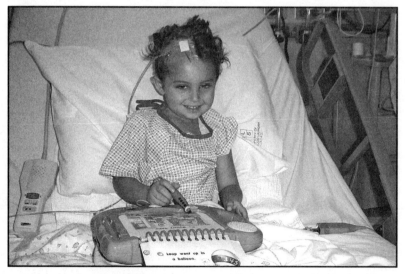

Mark's son, Mason, after surgery to remove a brain tumor.

Surgery was the next day. The doctor warned us that Mason might lose full use of his arms and legs. He might not be able to walk.

Fortunately, he survived that surgery, but a couple weeks later, he was back in surgery to drain water on his brain. After another week in the hospital, the pressure in his brain started to come down. Our boy was getting better. The hospital released him, and we brought him home. He still could not walk and, while we hoped for the best, we knew what the worst could be.

Over time, he got better.

For the next five years, Mason had regular MRIs. He was one worried little boy each time they wired him up back in the hospital. It felt to him as if it were all happening again. We were told that if he made it for five years without incident, he would be considered cured. In 2009, five years arrived. Mason was declared cured.

And then one night my wife Ivette and I were out to dinner at our friend Jack Daly's house. We had left our phones in the car so that no calls would interrupt our time together. When we returned to the car, we found dozens of messages. Mason was back in the hospital. He had been playing at a friend's house, and he'd had multiple seizures.

In the years before, during, and after the initial surgeries, Mason had never had a seizure.

That evening, Mason was transferred back to Children's Hospital of Orange County, where brain monitors indicated hundreds of seizures. After several days of brain activity tests, however, the doctors concluded that the seizures were psychogenic in origin. They were self-created.

In therapy, Mason told us that he was just tired of all those doctors and hospitals and white coats. When he was younger, we could tell how scared he was—even if he didn't tell us, we could see it in his eyes. Now, he was telling us outright what he thought about it all. He was done with it.

"Look, Mason," my wife said to him one day, "whatever demons you have in your stomach, why don't you give them to me, and together we'll throw them in the trash can." And they did. He has not had a seizure since.

Ivette and I had different ways of dealing with Mason's illness. I was task-list oriented. She had a lot more of an emotional response. When it comes to healing, there is a place for both.

In the end, our family gained strength from the ordeal. I do not doubt that Mason is a stronger young man because of what he endured and overcame. And I know that our marriage benefited as we learned to deal with our differences and, together, gained a perspective on what really matters in life.

Challenges such as we faced can be so consuming that they truly test a marriage. A marriage can get stronger, or it can dissolve into divorce. We committed to get stronger. And to this day, we make it a practice to devote time to each other—a week together, just the two of us, at least every quarter of the year.

Today, Mason is healthy and happy. He had some problems with motor skills for a while but no cognitive consequences. He has been able to be a regular kid. He has faced other challenges in life—including exciting ones that he has eagerly pursued. Mason is showing the world that life doesn't just happen to him.

If Mason was one scared little boy, I was certainly one scared daddy, too. I had always been the guy who could work hard and get results. I could make things happen—but this was outside of my control. It was humbling. His tumor was the size of a golf ball. Most such tumors are malignant, and the surgery doesn't end well. In his case, we got the desired results—and it certainly was not my doing.

Top: Mason completing the Antarctica Marathon at 14 years old.

Bottom: Mason running the 8k at the Great Wall of China.

GIVE BACK

As Mason was recovering, I felt a deep sense of gratitude. I felt the desire to give back. In my business career, I have long believed that the people who think big and who act big are the ones who will be big. I decided to take my own advice. To raise money for Children's Hospital of Orange County, where Mason was treated, I decided to compete in the Ironman Canada triathlon.

Even before Mason became ill, I had been participating in short, sprint triathlons and was enjoying them. Afterward, having seen how much had been done for our son, I decided to do something big: I was going to do an Ironman triathlon as a tribute to the doctors, with a goal to raise $100,000 for the hospital. I wanted to donate the proceeds to the neurosciences group.

When I set this goal for myself, I wasn't exactly in shape. Around the time our kids were born, I was a golfer, not a triathlete. In fact, I weighed twenty-five pounds more then. I resolved to get into shape. I hired a top triathlon coach for about eighteen months of training. The training was arduous, as one might expect for a competition that includes a 2.4-mile swim, a 112-mile bike ride, and a 26.2-mile run—which is a full marathon—all in one day.

Through it all, I kept sight of why I was doing this: to support the hospital that saved our son's life and was in the business of saving many lives. And I was doing it in honor of Mason. I knew that what I was enduring in training was nothing compared with what he had endured.

I chose to do this Ironman in Canada because, after all, I am a native Canadian. The whole family joined me there in August 2006, and we all wore shirts that said "Ironman for Mason and CHOC." We set up a webpage for donations and raised $110,000 for the hospital.

Left: Mark, with family, after completing Ironman Canada.
Right: With friends and Mason after completing Ironman Switzerland.

I finished my first Ironman in twelve hours and fifty-five minutes. In the final stretch, I began to cry. I knew that Mason would be waiting for me near the end of the course and that we were going to be running to the finish line together.

If you believe in yourself, you can achieve anything you want in life. That's the power of Ironman. Since that day, I have tried to inspire many others to get involved in Ironman, to push themselves to be their best. A friend and client of mine, Eric Crews from Boston, managed to drop seventy pounds to get in shape for his first Ironman. Together, he and I completed Ironman Switzerland. My friends Chris Jannuzzi and Brandon Ames dropped forty and fifty pounds, respectively, and completed the race as well. Eric needed two IVs when he finished but managed to join us a few hours later for a beer. Mason competed in the kids swim/run too. My goal is to compete on every continent. I have done a dozen of these events—including five Hawaii Ironman World Championships.

I continue to devote myself to other activities that are deeply meaningful to me. I spend time with family. I advocate for children's fundraisers. I speak around the world about my experiences.

I view life not as what I have to do but as what I get to do. Today, I get to help CEOs worldwide build their businesses and achieve their dreams. Every day, I get to make a difference. Every day, that inspires me.

Like Ironman competitors, businesspeople, too, need to think and act big if they are to rise above the crowd and *make BIG happen*! Those few who have been spared hardship must listen well to those who have been tempered by adversity. The world of business demands leaders with an iron spirit.

PERSPECTIVE

Mason's brain tumor made me feel powerless. In other hardships in my life, I felt an element of control. I could take some sort of action. I could cut my losses. Life would carry on. But this was

Competing in all phases of the Hawaii Ironman World Championship.

our little boy lying in the hospital bed. Would his life carry on? And if it didn't, how could we?

The only thing we could control during that time was ourselves. We couldn't control the outcome, but we could control our attitude toward the challenge given to us. I would not dwell on the negatives. I would focus on and expect a positive outcome.

The ordeal that our family faced with Mason gave us the gift of perspective. When I hear acquaintances complaining about the utter nonsense in their daily lives, I sometimes offer to take them over to the children's hospital for a tour of the cancer floor. Nobody has taken me up on it, but I'm sure they get the point.

When I was chairman of our Young Presidents Organization chapter, in 2007, I decided to have an event at the children's hospital. We watched from a viewing room as surgeons performed brain tumor surgery on a twelve-year-old girl. The doctors wore cameras on their eye scopes so that we could see up close the same things that they were seeing. We all wore microphones so we could carry on a discussion during the surgery. Mostly, we were silent as we watched in awe.

At one point, one of the doctors asked, "Hey, Mark, everyone all right in there? You guys aren't saying much." I'm sure we were not. Considering that they had a little girl's brain open in front of them, it hardly seemed the time for casual conversation.

As we watched the surgery, it all seemed rather clinical, as if we were watching a documentary. But afterward, when they had stitched her up and removed the wrappers from her head, we could see her little face and blond hair, and we gasped. This was no documentary. This was life. A few minutes later, the surgeons came in to see us— and this was a room full of CEOs who, for once, had little to say.

In any life, we'll all experience the days of desolation, as well as the ones of sparkling inspiration. I have come to understand that what comes our way often is a matter of what we have come to expect. And I have learned firsthand how the dreary days give us an appreciation for the dreamy ones.

There will always be surprises, but what matters most is how you learn from the experience, accept it for what it is, and apply it. Now, in everything I do, I try to have fun and to influence others positively. I have reached the point in life where I get to do that every day. I strive to make a difference. That is the greatest form of success.

BELIEVE

The theme for this book is "*Make Big Happen*!" You will succeed when you believe in yourself. I know it, Mason knows it, and anyone who has endured adversity knows it. As long as you stay in the game, anything is possible.

Resources

ABOUT CEO COACHING INTERNATIONAL

CEO Coaching International helps entrepreneurs and CEOs increase profitability, drive margin growth, and gain accountability. We guide you to grow your business and achieve your goals.

We know the intensity, focus, and commitment it takes to be a successful entrepreneur and CEO. The CEO Coaching International team has decades of experience building and selling successful businesses, leading fast-growing organizations, and driving sales and revenue to create industry-leading results.

Today, we coach dozens of the world's top entrepreneurs and CEOs who want to increase profitability and accelerate growth. We deliver top-rated speaking engagements for more than 7,500 CEOs, business leaders, and executives from more than eighty countries.

Our clients have experienced, on average, 266 percent profit growth while working with CEO Coaching International. How is this triple-digit growth possible? There are four key reasons:

1.   Methodology

Our simple best practices methodology allows coaches to quickly assess the steps that must be taken and help CEOs put an execution plan in place. This no-nonsense, bottom line approach enables organizations to see real results quickly. When we engage clients in coaching, these questions frame our conversations and ensure we stay focused on what generates the results our clients desire. We call them The Make Big Happen Questions. They are:

    a. What do you want? **(Vision)**

    b. What do you have to do? **(Action)**

    c. What could get in the way? **(Anticipate)**

    d. How do you hold yourself accountable? **(Measure)**

2.   Accountability

Employees are all held accountable for their responsibilities, but when a CEO or entrepreneur makes a commitment, who holds him or her accountable? Coaching creates accountability and allows CEOs and entrepreneurs to follow through on what they know they need to do. For example, the CEO of a billion-dollar line of business within a multibillion-dollar corporation unexpectedly resigned, and the new CEO was given a challenge by the board to turn the company around within six months. The new CEO recognized the need for objective feedback and accountability and turned to an executive coach to help him achieve his objectives. With the help of expert and committed coaching, the CEO achieved his goals and increased revenues, reduced costs, and reestablished profitability to the line of business within six months.

3.   Identify Blind Spots

Everyone has blind spots—damaging behaviors that everyone but ourselves can see clear as day. For CEOs, these blind spots create unwelcome consequences. They corrupt decision-making, reduce the scope of awareness, and sabotage business results. Blind spots are also less obvious when things are going well. It is very easy for executives to become almost strictly inward looking, especially when they have been very successful. But these blind spots can become devastating when performance moves in the other direction. A good, neutral third-party assessment is a clear reality check for executives.

4.   Strategic Relationships

The coaches at CEO Coaching International are an experienced roster of CEO A-listers, each with the ability to introduce a client to key people that will help his or her business. The coaches have decades of experience as successful CEOs and entrepreneurs and have access to otherwise unattainable resources that enable our clients to better achieve objectives.

In addition to coaching, we offer the following:

1. ## Employee assessment tools.

    Using the right assessment tools can make the difference between a great hire and a disastrous one. We offer the DISC system and behaviors and motivators to aid you in the process of hiring candidates as well as assessing existing employees.

2. ## Planning meeting facilitation.

    Our coaches are experts at facilitating quarterly and annual strategy meetings.

3. ## Keynote speaking.

    With years of in-the-trenches experience, our coaches speak on a variety of topics designed to inspire your team and provide them with practical, actionable ideas they can implement immediately.

To learn more, please visit CEOCoachingInternational.com, or call us at 1-866-622-9583.

ON YOUR MARK, GET SET, GROW! PODCAST

Launched in early 2015, the CEO Coaching International podcast focuses on helping entrepreneurs and CEOs grow their business, develop their people, and elevate their own performance.

As an interview-based show, we speak to leading entrepreneurs and CEOs who share how they succeeded, what they learned from their failures, and the best practices that led them to build world-class companies.

Here are a few examples of past shows:

1. From 2 to 4500 Employees: How a 29-year-old entrepreneur built the startup that all startups need.

2. Chuck Davis, storied CEO, e-commerce pioneer, and past international chairman of YPO, shares a lifetime of business lessons.

3. Medical entrepreneur Leslie Michelson discusses the most critical factors most CEOs pay little attention to.

4. Former Tony Robbins and Richard Branson colleague, Scott Duffy, talks on marketing, thinking big, and launching new products.

5. Fifteen-time Ironman finisher, serial entrepreneur, and top sales trainer Jack Daly shares seven hard-earned business lessons learned from being an Ironman.

6. Seasoned entrepreneurs reveal the biggest lessons they learned from decades of in-the-trenches experience starting and selling businesses.

7. A humbled entrepreneur reflects on six key lessons he learned in turning his company around from near bankruptcy to a thriving $300 million business.

8. Top entrepreneurs share proven ways to help leaders make better and more profitable executive decisions.

9. How to sell your business to a strategic buyer and get up to 300 percent more money for it.

10. Six strategies an entrepreneurial Boston firm used to achieve massive growth and a huge exit.

11. How to hire top performers so you can ignite growth.

12. The five things every CEO should focus on.

13. The difference between a good salesperson and a great one.

14. How transparency in communication makes you a better leader.

To subscribe for free, simply visit the CEOCoachingInternational.com website or access the show via the podcast app on your smartphone.